CH0068836 4

2ND BATTALION
THE ESSEX REGIMENT
"THE POMPADOURS"
'D' DAY TO 'VE' DAY
IN NORTH WEST EUROPE

The Naval & Military Press Ltd

Published by

The Naval & Military Press Ltd
Unit 10 Ridgewood Industrial Park,
Uckfield, East Sussex,
TN22 5QE England

Tel: +44 (0) 1825 749494
Fax: +44 (0) 1825 765701

www.naval-military-press.com
www.nmarchive.com

With Acknowledgements to
W i l l i a m S h a k e s p e a r e
for all photograph captions.

FOREWORD

This Booklet represents only a page in the long history of the POM-PADOURS, but I feel that it is a page which bears comparison with all the other brilliant episodes in the past.

It is not intended to be an official account, but a short story of events during the Campaign in North West Europe. It is the result of contributions by many who were with the Battalion during operations and whose memories are still fresh. It will serve its purpose if, in the days to come, it will be a reminder for those who have left us of a happy and successful association and for those who come to join us an inspiration to perpetuate the spirit of the POMPADOURS in the future.

V. C. Magill-Cuerdon.

PREFACE

Writing the story of the Battalion's activities in the North West European campaign of 1944/45 has been a happy task. Often I had to ask other Officers and ORs to correct my impressions of certain battles and less unpleasant incidents — and together we have recalled and smiled over what "Old So-and-So did and said". The whole idea of this little story is just that. Poor though it may be, it is intended to be something that we can all retain and eventually take home with us and in the years to come, when we meet and start talking of old times, we shall be able to get out this history and have a ready guide to the sequence of events. Maybe in our bath-chairs we shall even read extracts to our grand children with pride in our hearts and complete boredom in theirs. For it is right that we should have pride in our hearts. Nothing which was asked of us was not done, never were the men dispirited but always one could be sure that one would be met with a smile and confidence in the ability to overcome all difficulties, whatever they might be. There is no need for me to say that we have been the happiest of bands, the two special Orders reproduced later in this book put it in far better words than I can summon and above all, you who were a part of that band, know it to be true. The most difficult part in writing a history such as this, is to obtain a detached viewpoint and in this I must ask your forbearance if you feel that some particular incident is poorly recounted and much important data omitted. You will say that this story deals almost exclusively with the Rifle Coys.: but I would emphasise that rarely did a Rifle Coy. operate without its Carrier Sections, Pioneer and Anti-Tank Gun detachments and unsupported by 3" Mortars. Never has a Battalion been better served by its Signal Platoon. I could name all the departments and eulogise on their splendid service but Lt. Col. Scott's Special Order, reprinted at the end of this booklet, does it for me and it is only necessary to reiterate that our successes have been the result of team work in which all have had their part to play and have played it to the full. Finally, some of our friends in the other Arms of the Service which have either been "Under Command" or "In Support" may feel hurt that no reference has been made to them. Here I would say that this little history has been written by the Battalion, of the Battalion, for the Battalion and that we have felt that the Gunners, the Sappers and all the other Units who have worked with us, were a part of the family and have made equal contribution to the cause. Many of them will know that it was genuine pleasure that we showed when we met in the field and that we are still very happy when they come along to see us now.

A. A. VINCE.

1

BATTALION OFFICERS. Taken at CHRISTCHURCH shortly before D Day

(Rear Row) Lt. Price, Lt. Harris, Lt. Smith, Lt. Veale, Lt. Whitton, Lt. Bell, Lt. Haxell, Lt. Whitley, Lt. Cooper, Lt. Miller, Lt. Murphy.
(Centre) Capt. Barry, Lt. Grigg, Lt. Hetherington, Capt. Smyter, Lt. Butler, Lt. Kitch, Capt. Hearne, Lt. Vince, Lt. Cannon, Lt. Spencer, Capt. Alexander, Lt. Filby.
(Front) Capt. Frier, Capt. Chell, Major Barras, Major Watson, Major Elliot, Lt. Col. Higson MC, Capt. Townrow, Major Holme, Capt. Wilkins, Capt. Hale, Capt. Needham.

2

THE PREPARATIONS

In this effort to portray the magnificent part played by "The Pompadours" in the resounding victory over the Wehrmacht in 1944/45, we have called it 'D' Day to 'VE' Day; but obviously the story starts long before the ramps of our invasion craft went down on the beaches of NORMANDY on 6 June 1944. It starts about the end of February 1944; the Battalion had returned wet and muddy and still half frozen from "Exercise Eagle", one of the many pre-invasion exercises in which we took part. We returned to DURHAM only to pack up and sever our connections with 47 (London) Division with its familiar and well liked Bow Bells flash. We said good bye to our untold friends in the Cathedral City which had taken us so generously into its homes. We had our last drinks at the "Three Tuns" and the "Cock-of-the-North" and, as February ended, we moved into Clacton-on- Sea in our own County.

A very different CLACTON to the one we knew in peace time. The bomb-damaged town, the mined and wired-off sea front, the rows of houses militarily requisitioned, the closed cinemas and shops all seemed bent on depressing us. By now it was pretty generally known that our days as an "Admin." Bn. were over and that we were destined to be part of the initial invasion force for the assault on the Fortress of Europe. Much hard work still seperated us from 'D' Day and officially the period at CLACTON was supposed to cover mobilisation in all its forms. We stayed there for 25 days equipping and being brought up to strength and all the time we marched and shot and threw grenades and carried out Platoon and Company schemes. It was in this area that 56 Infantry Brigade was formed, comprised of three regular Battalions, 2nd. Bn. The Gloucestershire Regt., 2nd. Bn. The South Wales Borderers and 2nd. Bn. The Essex Regt.

On 25 March we moved by train to INVERARY to undergo 10 days at the Combined Training Centre there. The country was beautiful and the training interesting though arduous. We played with all the known forms of invasion craft, clambered up and down scrambling nets, roared ashore and made "beachheads", turned "beachheads" into "bridgeheads", broke out from "bridgeheads" and we soon began to realise that only our presence was necessary to ensure the reconquest of EUROPE!! On 31 March we said goodbye to Lt. Col. L. W. W. Marriott as he relinquished command of the Battalion to Lt. Col. J. F. Higson MC,

4 April found us back in the South of England, this time in the area of CHRISTCHURCH with less than two months to put the finishing touches to our preparations. Here was the final sort out in men and materials and the continuance of our battle training. In anticipation of the speed with which we intended to march through NORMANDY we hardened our feet by tramping 100 miles through the HAMPSHIRE Countryside in 7 days. All the possible small arms and grenade practice that could be crammed in was done in conjunction with the eternal right or left flankers, the frontal assault, the withdrawal, the relief, the approach to contact and everything that the book enumerated. Here we carried out more and more invasion exercises such as "SMASH" and "FABIUS". It was at the latter that the sad accident occurred when Major Norman Ayres and 6 ORs were drowned whilst wading out to re-embark on our invasion barges.

3

Whilst all this aggressive training was going on, the C. O., Lt. Col. J. F. Higson MC, the 2 I. C., Major G. G. Elliott, and the Adjutant, Captain J. Townrow, were working behind locked doors on mysterious "Top Secret" documents. These were the only people in the Battalion who knew the venue of the coming party and they were the officers who finally decided the loading tables so carefully experimented with and suggested by the Company Commanders. The boat loads used in "SMASH" and "FABIUS" provided the basis for the actual operation although we "Guinea Pigs" did not know that at the time.

For some months now leave had been stopped and on 19 May 1944 we had to relinquish our last bit of freedom when we went behind barbed wire in Camp B 3 near BEAULIEU in Hampshire. This was to be our home under canvas for exactly 15 days before embarkation. 15 days of boredom which was only lightly relieved by the small amount of training and sport allowed by our confined surroundings and the occasional convivial evening in celebration of the days to come. Here it was we received our 24 — hour packs, our Mae Wests and all the hundred and one articles that go to make up an invasion force. Here we were let into the secret of operation "BIGOT NEPTUNE" — the invasion of NORMANDY. We learnt that 56 Infantry Brigade was to be an independent Brigade attached to 50 (Northumbrian) Division who were to assault the beaches of ARROMANCHES, some six miles North of the town of BAYEUX. That we were to land some two or three hours after the first wave and extend the "Beachhead" into a "Bridgehead" and go all out for BAYEUX. Days were spent memorizing maps, vertical and oblique air photos, models which showed every detail of country and known defence. As yet we were ignorant of the exact location of the assault for all place names had been given codewords. "PITTSBURG" for BAYEUX and "ODESSA" for the little fishing port of Le. HAMEL are two examples.

ENLARGING THE BRIDGEHEAD.

On 3 June 1944 the Battalion embarked at Lymington on to Landing Craft Infantry (Large). These craft are capable of taking just short of 200 ·men and so we had approximately one and a half companies on each vessel. The L. C. Is were Canadian, and the food 14 man pack Compo. — rations which we were going to endure for a long time. Anxiously we watched the sky as the wind came up and hurriedly we made quickly available our bags vomiting and enquired for anti-sea sickness pills. That night we tied up in Southampton Docks and learned that the operation was postponed for 24 hours. However we were on the ships and on the ships we were forced to stay, though subsequently we were allowed on to the quay-side for games, exercise and the eternal "Char and Wads" at the canteens which had been set up for us.

In the late evening of 5 June we cast off and slowly moved down Southampton Water to take up our positions in the greatest mass of shipping ever known in this world. To us on board, it seemed that had the opposition been able to bomb, they would have had almost a dry land target — so closely packed was the invasion fleet. Darkness fell before we reached the open sea and below decks, jammed like sardines in a tin, we drank our tins of self-heating soup and cocoa and played a little pontoon or housy-housy before trying to get a few hours sleep before the Great Day dawned.

We slept well that night without a worry; but the morning light of 6 June 1944 found us very shaken by the rolling and pitching of our ship. Many of us were violently sea-sick but those that were able went on deck and, as the light begun to improve, we could make out the coast of FRANCE. It all seemed strangely quiet. The bombers had finished their missions on the beach defences, the Airborne troops were in NORMANDY and the assault Battalions of 50 Div. were ashore and either still fighting on the beaches or smashing their way inland. The sea was very rough and, in the miserable and cloudy sky, Lightnings and Spitfires patrolled over our convoy which crawled and circled towards the shore. Clouds of smoke could be seen billowing upwards from the land and Battleships and Cruisers, Destroyers and rocket-firing Craft were still pouring fire into the defences and lines of approach. Occasionally a sea mine would float by and as the morning progressed, we began to struggle into our equipment as best we could in the crowded decks. We put on waterproof over-trousers and discarded them immediately, for we should never have got ashore in such cumbersome garments laden as we were. The odd tin of selfheating soup was tucked away in battle-dress blouses and the M. O. helped us to waterproof our watches.

As midday approached the craft nosed their way into the land and we could see plainly the coast line. Something akin to consternation was caused when we found that we could not reconcile the appearance of the land with the models we had memorised in Camp B3. Le HAMEL, where we were due to land, was still not free and it was thus necessary to go ashore some mile and a quarter to the East. The sea held much evidence of tragedies already enacted, wrecked landing craft and vehicles, disabled tanks, floating compo boxes and items of equipment. At 1225 hours the leading craft grounded, the ramps went down and the men streamed ashore. Some into water only knee deep, others up to their necks but all made dry land, crossed the short stretch of shingle and clambered over the low sea wall. A quarter of a mile to the left our transport, including all "S" Company vehicles, was having a much more difficult time. Mines were encountered by the score and the few clear lanes were blocked by bogged or "drowned" lorries and tanks. The sea wall, low though it was, increased the problems but somehow all were overcome. According to plan, we formed up in boat-loads and moved off to the prearranged assembly area near RYES, some 2¹/₂ miles inland. On the rising ground to our left we could see a long line of Shermans forming up and and we gasped as we saw that they were parked almost head to tail. As we marched along we saw and heard German beach defences still holding out but our orders were to get inland and we pushed on. Past small batches of prisoners we went, through minefields already gapped. Numbers of dead and wounded from both sides littered the roads, some hurriedly but efficiently dressed by the SBs but others as yet untouched and we could not help them. The roads along which we marched

5

EARLY DAYS
".... this great work,
Which is, almost, to
pluck a kingdom down,
And set another up."

6

were now being shelled by 75s at short range but casualties were few and soon we came to the assembly area, quickly deployed and dug in for the first time. The area was in a small wood not entirely clear and the odd sniper was still operating. A row of large poplars caused us some trouble until a Sherman came up and one by one picked off the tree tops where the snipers were concealed. In the early afternoon we checked up and found that apart from a Signals 15 cwt., 'A' Company's No. 1 15 cwt. and the Pioneers' Jeep which had been drowned, we were all present. The initial stage in ·the de-waterproofing of vehicles was carried out, Mae Wests discarded and we were ready for the first job — the capture of BAYEUX, a large and important road and rail Cathedral City, some 6 miles from the coast and almost due South of ARROMANCHES.

At 1600 hours the Commanding Officer gave the word and 'A' Company led off on the road to BAYEUX. 9 Platoon were in the van mounted on the Carrier Platoon's vehicles and they made all possible speed followed more sedately by 7 and 8 platoons and Company HQ mounted on airborne cycles. Only isolated and bewildered Boche were encountered and without exception these decided that discretion was really the better part and they also turned South and ran. With the 2nd. Bn. the South Wales Borderers and the 2nd. Bn. The Gloucestershire Regt. progressing equally well on the flanks, the day continued to go astonishingly according to plan but darkness fell with the leading elements still $1^1/_4$ miles from the city. There we dug in and during the night patrols went out to look at the anti-tank ditch surrounding BAYEUX. In the gathering dusk, as we looked at the spires of the Cathedral, it seemed that the city was almost undefended and the returning patrols confirmed this. Even so it would have been a brave man who would have suggested that we should take BAYEUX almost without a shot being fired; and to save being sorry afterwards, a limited left flanking attack was laid on. At 1100 hours on 7 June, 'A' Company went in supported by tanks of the Sherwood Rangers. Only a little sniping in the streets developed and the offenders were quickly liquidated. By 1300 hrs. the town was secure, the Companies deployed defensively and the inhabitants sufficiently recovered from the shock to commence looting the German QM's stores. Now we received our introduction to Calvados, that fiery spirit resulting from distilling cider and named after the department of France from which it originates. A tank threat on the right flank caused a redeployment of our 6-pounder anti-tank guns and PIATs but it was written off before reaching us and soon we were on the move Southward again. That night we reached a little feature South of Le LOUP HORS without incident and dug in on either side of the main road to the South. In the late evening we had our first meal in FRANCE, small though it was, and a few marauding Dorniers made it advisable to keep close to one's slit trench.

So far we had bumped no real opposition and the next two days brought no material change. It seemed to us that the Boche were badly disorganised and some of their units could have little idea of where the front actually was, for a motor cycle combination drove slap into our lines and after a sharp engagements two of the three passengers were taken prisoner and the third liquidated more decisively. A German press correspondent also drove into 'C' Company's area and was most surprised to find that he could not return. We held this feature for two days and the time was invaluable to us. We cleaned up and checked over our weapons, the balance of our vehicles were landed and joined us and, apart from a small residue of "Luxury" vehicles, we were up to scale.

In the late evening of 9 June we were relieved and spent a wet night in the fields near BAYEUX before coming under command of 7 Armoured Division (The Desert Rats) on the following day. Before first light we were off again and by midday we had put several miles between ourselves and BAYEUX. We paused for several hours near the village of ELLON whilst the "I" people decided where the opposition really was. Some stray Champagne helped to cheer us up and then we heard that the enemy were holding the Monastery at JUAYE MONDAYE, a most substantial building little more than a mile from our own positions. By now we were in typical Bocage country — small fields with extremely thick hedges, scattered woods and sunken roads and footpaths with everything in favour of the defender and nothing to help the attacker who must crash through all the obstacles and never see the enemy who waits until he cannot miss. Through such country 'D' Company attacked JUAYE MONDAYE after a considerable artillery preparation. Even now the enemy had not recovered from his initial shock, and as we advanced in extended line, he ran for the shelter of the woods to his rear and only a few snipers remained to worry us together with cross fire from Spandaus in the woods. The monastery area was quickly cleared but the Boche made some pretence of standing in these woods and there was little future in putting one's head above the level of banks or ditches. Again quite a sizeable piece of ground had been won at the cost of only a few casualties.

ESSEX WOOD AND TILLY-SUR-SEULLES.

So we came to Sunday 11 June — the first of a succession of Sundays characterised by bloody attacks, costly but always victorious. As yet the Allied grip on North West Europe was no more than a toe-hold and even we, the most advanced troops on the British right flank, were little more than 7 miles inland. But that small strip of land was an incredible sight to the drivers and "quarter-blokes" who went daily back to the beaches for food and materials of war. Mulberry Harbour was operating and an increasing variety of small craft were ferrying ashore colossal reserves of all kinds, both in anticipation of the breakout and also in case the weather, already bad, should turn for the worse and prevent work on the beaches completely. Air Strips for A. O. P. planes and even Spitfires were in use and every field, orchard and lane held dumps of ammunition, food, petrol and reserve weapons. So congested, albeit orderly, was the area, that camouflage was already a thing of the past. The bridgehead was still raked with German shellfire and casualties on the beaches had a worrying time before they could be evacuated to England. Out at sea, British Battleships pumped their terrifying shells ahead of our forward troops. Names like WARSPITE, RENOWN and NELSON were to figure in our operation orders under the heading of "supporting fire" for many days to come.

Leaving JUAYE MONDAYE to the care of the Recce Regiment, we detoured to the South and around midday on 11 June we were some 1¹/₂ miles from VERRIERES WOOD with the little village of the same name nestling in the woods. It was known that the Boche were holding the place in some strength and an afternoon attack was planned, supported on the flanks by the tanks of the Desert Rats. However something went wrong with the A. F. V. support and the attack that started at 1500 hours was purely an Infantry affair. The start line was taped on the South side of some particularly close country and in front of 'A' and 'C' Companies as they formed up was a ripening cornfield 1000 yards deep with VERRIERES WOOD at the far end. Barely a sound disturbed the warm Sunday afternoon but, as we moved off on a compass bearing, our own supporting artillery opened up. 25-pounders shelled the forward edges of our objective, superimposed with medium and, to the rear, enemy lines of communication and suspected enemy positions were pounded by mediums and guns of the Fleet.

Both "A" and "C" Companies attacked with two platoons up with the third Platoon and Company HQ in the centre and 50 yards to the rear. Even now it is easy to picture the attack. Ahead were the dark threatening woods and under the June sun the Infantry advanced at the rate of 100 yards everey two minutes through the gently bending golden corn. It was a picture book frontal assault and the line of attacking men kept perfect formation with Major Holme of "A" Company and Major Barrass of "C" Company in the lead. Half way through that cornfield, it seemed that it was to be another piece of cake for so far nothing had come back — but our hopes were very shortlived. In front of us the forward spraying 25-pounder shells were suddenly screened by the all-round burst of German heavy mortars interspersed with artillery and 88mm tank guns firing H. E. So far the bursts were still some 150 yards away but the fire was intensely accurate and obviously visibly controlled as the shells and bombs continued to burst with sickening regularity across the whole length of "A" Company's and part of "C"'s front. Through that deadly barrage the men advanced at a walk with rifles and automatics at the hip shooting into the woods beyond. As every salvo dropped on the thin line, we went flat on the ground while shell fragments cut lanes through the corn like scythes. In a second we were on our feet again but as we neared the wood the gaps were becoming very apparent and looking back towards the supporting Companies, one could see many rifles upturned in the ground indicating the spot where men had fallen, some never to rise again, others beyond the stage of "Walking Wounded".

As we began to cross the last 100 yards of meadow-land that seperated the corn from the woods, spandaus and rifles added their weight to the enemy artillery and mortars but once again the opposition refused the bayonet and withdrew from the forward edge to the farm buildings just beyond our objective. On the objective, our troubles were only just begining, for we were being raked by automatics at short range from the cover of the buildings. Down in the dip, a couple of fields away, some Tiger Tanks, ignoring any pretence at concealment, were turning their 88's and M. Gs on our line. 7 Platoon under Lt. Filby, now at less than half strength, brilliantly cleared the farms whilst 'B' Company coming up in support, quickly flushed some orchards and cottages, during which operation

9

the commander, Major Watson, was wounded and had to be evacuated. On the right "C" Company were now supported by "D" Company and this flank was firmly held though Major Petre, commanding the latter Company, had been killed in the attack. The counterattack came very quickly but was limited, fortunately for us, almost entirely to tanks. Unsupported by our own tanks or A/Tank guns our only answer was PIATs and "A" Company found that all their three PIAT men were out of action. Two of these weapons had been salvaged but the bomb supply was insufficient to make any impression on the Tigers and they broke right into our positions. No ground was given but it was often necessary to side step to avoid being run over. Seemingly the Tigers were running short of H. E. for they were firing solid shot and, terrifying though this is, it does little damage to Infantry. "B" Company suffered badly at this stage, for besides many killed and wounded they lost two whole platoons who were surrounded and taken prisoner. "D" Company, who had been ordered to divert troops to help "B", found Tigers well behind our forward positions and they sustained terrible casualties without being able to do anything about it. Doubts about our own tanks and guns must have worried the Tigers, for this can be the only reason why they relinquished their moral and material advantage and withdrew to the cover of VERRIERES VILLAGE, leaving us in sole possesion of the battlefield.

The short remaining period of daylight allowed us to make limited adjustments to our positions and all the time both sides continued to shell the opposition. Away in front of us, enemy tanks would come up under cover of the bocage hedgerows, shell and withdraw again whilst all the time we could hear the rumble of heavy Boche vehicles in the village until the mediums plastered the place and billowing columns of smoke told of a reduced threat. A more determined counterattack, this time comprised of men and Flame-throwers, came in about midnight. The shouting of German soldiers and the noise of their vehicles was the only indication until the searing jet of flame was thrown amongst us and men lying wounded in the fields were unable to evade this terrifying weapon. The situation became so confused that the only answer was to bring artillery down on to our own positions and for twenty minutes regiments of 25-pounders flooded the area with fire. Again the Boche withdrew and once more we were left in undisputed possession of VERRIERES WOOD.

It seemed ages before dawn came to end the nightmare of 11/12 June but during that time the remains of the Battalion was organised into Composite Companies and the defensive layout completely tightened up. M. 10s and our own 6-pounder A/Tank guns were up by first light and out of chaos emerged a respectable defensive position. All through 12 June we waited for the next attack which never came. Only continued shelling by artillery and harrassing fire from their tanks disturbed us. The R. M. O. and the Stretcher Bearers contiued their magnificent work for the wounded, the dead were buried and equipment, weapons and ammunition salvaged. That day Major G. G. Elliott assumed command of the Battalion, a position he held for well over 3 months during which time he enhanced to a high degree the admiration and respect in which we already held him.

At 2230 hours we were ordered to new positions near the tiny village of FOLLIOT where we came into reserve. Thus ended the battle bf VERRIERES WOOD and if you mention VERRIERES WOOD now, people will look at you in surprise, for that little piece of NORMANDY cluttered with graves, dead cattle, broken equipment and stenched in death, is forever renamed ESSEX WOOD. Looking back now, one remembers many things, the work of the S. B.s, Padre Thomas shielding the bodies of the wounded with his own — actions for which he subsequently was awarded the Military Cross — the Messerschmitt which crashed during the attack and the dismal efforts of a little group of men in "A" Company who tried to knock out a Tiger which was too close to depress its guns upon them. One remembers the efforts of Major Elliott to improve our plight, the grip Major Michael Holme kept on his dwindling men during the awful night, the flame throwers and Lt. Price who searched high and low for a PIAT to take them on; but we remember most of all the line of men who went into the bitterest of attacks still very green but never once wavering.

We stayed at FOLLIOT for three days but it was no picnic. The line was thinly held and though officially in reserve, we were merely echeloned back to give depth to the defence and Boche 88s and even rifle fire continued to annoy us. However we snatched a little badly needed sleep, food became more regular and we carved the stubble off our chins.

We reverted to the command of 50 Division and on the 16th took up new positions near the village of BUCEELS. Here the Battalion was reinforced and we spent a further three days in a largely defensive role with the inevitable patrols and twenty-fours hour a day watchfulness. On 19 June we again went over to the attack; this time to the East of ESSEX WOOD with the village of TILLY-SUR-SEULLES as the objective. TILLY was a pretty little place, nestling in some rolling country almost due South of BAYEUX and still not a dozen miles from the beaches and well within range of our Fleet guns. We reformed up for the attack on a reverse slope with "A" Company on the right and "D" Company on the left, each with two platoons up in normal fashion. Crawling to the crest of the hill, one could see the dense hedgerows in front with the brow of the next ridge shielding TILLY in the valley beyond. One troop of AVREs was in support and with the usual artillery we started off soon after midday with the main North/South road into TILLY as a guide. Again the enemy had perfect control of the ground through his pre-selected OPs and soon his shells found us, causing casualties but not hindering the advance. "D" Company continued to go well and obtained an insecure hold on the left edge of the straggling village but "A" Company were blocked efficiently on the final ridge. German MGs and rifles controlled the area and though many were flushed out of some farm buildings, they stuck grimly to the woods beyond and to go forward meant certain death. Casualties were mounting up from shellfire, small arms and mines and the leading Companies were ordered to dig in as the progress of the AVREs was made impossible by the presence of German 88s. "D" Company conformed to the positions of "A" Company and we then held roughly a crescent-shaped arc a little less than a mile from TILLY with a Battalion of the Durhams on our right. In the hot sunny day the stench of the dead swollen cattle was indescribable and incessant shelling and machine gunning made life very uncomfortable. Night came and went with no change in the stalemate position. Extensive patrolling confirmed no withdrawal by the enemy and the ensuing day still found no alteration. Sniping and shelling continued by both sides and dwindled as the day passed into a wet night. The day of the 21st brought torrential and continuous rain and at 1030 hrs we pulled out of our positions for a right flanking attack from the West through the Durhams. Many unsuccessful attempts had already been made to capture TILLY and as we wound our way through the battle-scarred lanes we saw plenty of evidence in the knocked-out Cromwell and Sherman tanks, the fewer German tanks and numbers of hastily dug graves. Not a building was untouched by war and as we came nearer to the village, every house was wrecked and broken. The securing of TILLY-SUR-SEULLES and the high ground beyond came as climax to the preceeding days, for the Boche had hastily withdrawn in front of us and "A" Company on the West saw only a handful of horribly wounded civilians until they met "B" Company, attacking from the North-East, in the centre of what was once a village. All kinds of mines and booby traps had been left to slow down our advance and several casualties were caused to the unwary who tried to enter houses without making sure that they were safe. We dug in once more in thick country on the ridge South of the village with the Boche in similiar positions on the far side of some open ground. The rest of the day was spent alternately in trying to rainproof our slit trenches and taking evasive action against exceedingly heavy "stonking" in which 88mm Ack Ack airbursts figured prominently. Casualties were not light.

On 22 June we were relieved and in sub-units we made our way back to ELLON where we rested for almost a week. Thus ended 16 days of unbroken action with practically no sleep. The seven mile march back was just about all we could manage but we had played our part in the enlargement of the bridgehead well and, more than that, we knew that the best the enemy could produce was not good enough. There had been cases of battle exhaustion in our ranks and over a third of the Battalion had been killed or wounded or posted as missing, but we were no longer green; rather were we troops who had been fully seasoned very quickly.

BOIS de ST GERMAIN to LAUNAY.

The stay at ELLON brought us may reinforcements and we ate, slept and went back to BAYEUX for a bath. Whilst some of our chaps were in BAYEUX, General "Monty" came along and wanted to see some "men from the ESSEX", a nice touch of recognition which we all appreciated. The weather was fair and in the best of form we relieved 6 GREEN HOWARDS in the line on 30 June 1944. The positions were in typical bocage country, innumerable hedgerows, copses, orchards and hidden lanes. A little over a mile to the South was the BOIS de ST GERMAIN with the small village of GRANVILLE on our right and in front the TILLY-HOTTOT-LA CHAPELLE lateral road which the German 7th Army was still defending fiercely. We were holding the extreme right of the British line with only 2 SWB between the Americans and ourselves. There the Battalion stayed for 8 days in indifferent weather. Battalion HQ was in a little whitewashed cottage still intact and the Companies dug into the

12

TILLY " . . . . . . Scarcely off a mile,
In goodly form, comes on the enemy."

banks and showed nothing to the enemy. 8 days of patrols and harrassing fire from our artillery, MMGs and 3" and 4.2" mortars with only negligible reply from the Boche.

On 7 July we received orders to secure the road in front of us and the surrounding woods comprising part of the BOIS de ST GERMAIN whilst 2 SWB on our right were to capture GRANVILLE. In support we had Shermans, MMGs and a troop of Crocodiles (flame-throwing Churchills) — a brand new weapon. Preparations continued throughout the 7th and during the following night we still patrolled to give the impression that nothing new was intended. Reveille was at 0300 hours on the 8th and at first light we were forming up in orchards occupied by the advanced companies and a bulldozer was smashing a path through the hedgerows for our vehicles to come up after the leading troops. As our barrage opened up there began another of our most bitter battles. The enemy were also preparing to attack and our shells tore into a Bn. of their 277 Infantry Brigade as it formed up on one of our objectives. As we found afterwards, the slaughter was incredible. Behind the barrage "A" Company once more led off and again had to pass through an enemy box of fire but casualties were light and 7 Platoon soon secured the cross-tracks which was their objective. 9 Platoon passed through and advanced eastwards along the main road but the tanks were unable to follow owing to mines

13

and they stayed on the North of the road giving covering fire. 9 Platoon then turned South and secured their objective with a left hook whilst 8 Platoon, pushing well to the left, put out a stop on the TILLY road. "C" Company now filled in the right of "A" Company whilst "B" and "D" Companies passed through and fought their way on to all the original objectives. The Battalion on the right was having a tough fight to approach GRANVILLE and we were ordered to dig in and sit tight.

We stuck there all that day and night under incessant shell and mortar fire and early in the morning of the 9th we could hear that for which we had been waiting — the preparations for a counter-attack. The shouting of German Officers and NCOs as they sorted out their men and the rumble of enemy tanks as they took up positions, came to us through the damp hazy first light. Artillery was quickly and accurately put on the forming-up places but the attack came in. Mark IV tanks, disguised as Tigers, bore down upon 7 Platoon and simultaneously hordes of infantry assailed "B", "D" and "A" Companies. For two hours the battle went on with both sides throwing in all the fire power of which they were capable and all that time the fighting was at the closest range. "D" Company repelled all their attacks and held grimly to their entire position. "B" Company took probably the main brunt of the effort and their line was dented but despite heavy casualties they reformed under Major Browne (who received the MC for his brilliant leadership in this battle) and they themselves counter attacked and restored the position. Meanwhile "A" Company on the right were hard pressed by tanks and infantry and the remnants of 7 Platoon were forced back from their crosstracks as a Mark IV completely wrote off a section and most of Platoon HQ. The German success was very shortlived. Lt Filby rallied his handful of men and reinforced by elements of "C" Company took on the tanks with PIATs. In the space of minutes three Mark IVs had been knocked out and the remainder with most of the accompanying infantry were in retreat.

There was little respite and we were shelled incessantly for the rest of the day but we evacuated our casualties, sent back the prisoners we had taken and adjusted our positions. We even had time to count eighty dead Boche only yards from "B" Company's positions. At 1800 hours the enemy put in his final attack, this time entirely on the bulge made by "B" and "D" Companies in the centre of the Battalion positions. The whole of the balance of the German Brigade was thrown in and yelling and firing they came across the fields right on to our automatics and rifles. Many were mown down but still they pressed the attack until the Crocodiles came up and wrought havoc in their decimated ranks. Gradually they broke and fled, chased by tongues of flame 150 yards long and by small arms fire. Apart from killed and wounded, we sent back over a hundred prisoners from this counter attack alone. That was the end of the battle of the BLOODY BOIS as far as we were concerned. The following day was wet and miserable and we, cold and tired, were relieved by a Battalion of the GREEN HOWARDS and returned to our original positions, though "C" Company remained under command of the relieving unit for a further night.

Any hopes we had of a short rest after the BOIS were soon dashed when, the following morning, we took over the positions of 2 GLOSTERS at

14

PARFOURU L'ECLIN. Here the Battalion held the extreme right of the British line for three weeks. On the right was a Texas Battalion and with them we manned joint posts. Need it be said that they fed better than we did and that it was a much sought after privilege to be part of the British patrol that worked in conjunction with the Yanks. On our left were 2 SWB and in front, 1000 yards of No-Man's-land with burnt-out farms, and shell-splattered fields and the endless dead and stinking cattle. To the rear of the forward Coys. and near Bn. HQ was the tiny village of Le PONT MULOT where, even now, one could still buy cider and freshly killed pork. Those of us who were with the Pompadours then will know that names such as LA COUARDE, TORTEVAL, LA BELLE EPINE (where the Sphinx Cinema first appeared) VILLERS BOCAGE and the like will live in our memory forever. We made no attacks whilst at PARFOURU but never the less it was a grim business. For every shell the Boche threw at us, the magnificent 50 Div. Artillery replied tenfold but the enemy remained undaunted. Particularly do we recall the SP guns that came in close, fired their complement of shells and withdrew again and the 150mm guns and larger that "stonked" the area day and night. We were told that we had to "lean" against the opposition and this meant patrols deep into enemy country by night and endless sniping by day. Patrols that were fraught with the utmost danger, for in addition to masses of mines and booby traps, the enemy consistently changed his positions. A farm or an orchard reported clear one night would be alive with Spandaus the next and a lane traversed by snipers by day would be mined and covered by fire at night. Here it was that Lt. Miller with a "D" Company patrol was ambushed within a couple of fields of our own positions. Less tragic was a patrol by Sjt. Skittrall who was ordered to recce LA COUARDE. Back in the Company slit trenches we heard the rattle of automatics from the objective and we waited, fearing the worst, until the patrol came back with a brace of hens riddled by Sten ammunition.

As July drew to a close a certain expectancy filled the air. On the left, the stumbling block of CAEN had been captured and fighting was going on beyond the town. 43 Div. joined 30 Corps and relieved the Texas Battalion on our right, freeing the Americans for the smash through to St. LO. Out in front, 2 Panzers had been relieved by a less formidable bunch and hostile shelling dwindled. The morning of 30 July was fine and we had a grand stand view of Lancasters and Halifaxes dropping over 1000 tons of HE on VILLERS BOCAGE, but the rest of that day and night and most of the 31st was passed in waiting whilst 2 GLOSTERS made limited attacks in front. The CO was summoned to Brigade at 1600 hours; at 1800 hours he gave his own orders for a full scale frontal assault on the stronghold of LAUNAY RIDGE to commence at 2000 hours. This seemed an awfully hurried affair after so much hanging about but like so many spontaneous efforts, it was crowned with incredible success. The Company Commanders dashed back to their men and gave orders for an immediate move and only as they marched to the start line were the Platoon Officers and NCOs. put in the picture. The star line was taped on the reverse slope of a ridge near the Burnt Out Farm and over the top of this ridge the ground dropped away across the main road to a wooded valley and rose steeply again to LAUNAY. Once in possession of LAUNAY RIDGE we could control the country for miles beyond and indeed óne could say that we would be out of the Bocage into the plains beyond. "A" Company were in the lead on the right with "B" on the left, supported respectively by "C" and "D".

At 2000 hours precisely the leading Companies moved off with 1¹/₂ miles to cover and with orders to secure the objectives by 2145 hours. Immediately in front of the start line was a minefield and it must be stated that most of us were sufficiently discreet to step in the footsteps of the man in front. However, once clear of this danger, we opened up into perfect formation again with the Company Commanders leading in the centre of their troops and keeping as little as twenty five yards behind a tremendous 25-pounder creeping barrage. 5.5 Howitzers, MMGs, Mortars and tanks added their fire power and overhead, Typhoons dived and blasted the Germans from their holes. The ground was covered at the rate of 100 yards every two minutes and regularly the word went back that all was going well.

On the hills to the rear, onlookers saw what was afterwards described as a perfect picture book attack. So we shall all remember it, as not once did the staggered line of Infantry pause as they climbed the last slope, firing from the hip as they went. Casualties were incredibly light and in front of us the Boche could stand it no longer. They broke and fled and it was a long time before they stopped running. Only a few remained behind their guns and these were soon killed or captured and at the stated time all Companies reported their objectives secured. The unkind may have said that the Boche never intended to hold LAUNAY that night but don't believe a word of it. Over 100 prisoners, 43 Spandous, brand new Panzerfausts, masses of small arms, indeed the entire equipment of two whole Battalions was the spoil we collected that evening and the next day. Their food was still in the pots and their mess tins and surely no one will say that the enemy left all this willingly?

This was to be our last show with 50 (N) Division and it was fitting that it should have been such a resounding success. We like to believe that the men from the North think as well of us as we do of the Northumbrian Battalions with whom we fought so many battles. On 1 August we were "pinched out" as other units exploited our success and pushed on into the open country. We stayed one more night at LAUNAY and the next day we went into rest near BUCEELS not far from the village of TILLY, now an open space from which the debris had been shovelled by bulldozers.

THE ORNE AND BAS BREUIL.

In lovely weather, we rested at BUCEELS for six days. Six days of beautiful sleep, washing and sunbathing. George Formby and his wife gave us our first Ensa show and we still laugh and talk about it to this day. There was a Brigade drumhead Service and we put on our own Battalion concert. Few of the still present will forget the Signals "Troubadours"; the Co, 2 IC and others playing "I want to be an actor" when Peter Butler had the dual role of settee and little dog, and Sjt. Newton gave the lads all their favourites on the piano. In the same programme in that small farmyard, the village priest sang a little thing called "La Petite Eglise"

16

and Pte Hayhow gave his inimitable rendering of "Buttercup Joe", not perhaps in quite the same taste but rather better received. And after that, led by Bill Barry, Den Grigg and John Kitch, we sang everything we knew including such old ditties as "The dogs they had a party" and something about a very large wheel.

The happy carefree days ended all too quickly and on 8 August we lost our status as an independent Brigade and joined 59 Infantry Division at a little place called LA FETERIE,, not very far West of the river ORNE, The same day we relieved another Brigade of our new Division near LA CAINE and spent that night in an orchard. The same night the ORNE was forced at heavy cost and a bridge secured by the WARWICKS and repaired and maintained by the Sappers. The following day we were ordered to cross the bridge at midnight and then turn South through the FORET de GRIMBOSQ in the direction of CROISILLES and FORGE-A-CAMBRO. As twilight turned into inky night we filed slowly along the road as it twisted and turned down the steep sides of the ORNE VALLEY and often we had to stop as tanks and supply vehicles also made their way to the one bridge. We crossed safely though the bridge was still being shelled and REs were still making good the holes where the shells fell. On the steep road on the East side we passed through the bridgehead Battalion and by a miracle we found our correct road in the chaos that existed. For four miles we advanced along that road to the South. On our left were the thick wooded slopes of the FORET de GRIMBOSQ and on the right the ground dipped sharply to the valley below. Every few yards at the side of the road were slit trenches hurriedly evacuated and every one had to be searched. Platoons of "A" Company took turns to lead the advance and a little before 0300 hours we reached a small village and silently checked every house before pushing on to the objective. Just before dawn we had a sharp engagement, wounding several and capturing an officer who died before reaching the RAP and, as the light improved, we began to dig in within a stone's throw of FORGE-A-CAMBRO which was burning fiercely. Four hundred yards away the Boche were also digging in and sniping developed. The forward Companies were on a reverse slope and suffered far less shelling than Battalion HQ and "S" Coy HQ a little way back. At 1100 hours on the morning of 10 August, "C" Company under Major Barrass put in a perfect attack on the Boche around FORGE-A-CAMBRO. Supported by Churchills, we went straight in and for the cost of only a few casualties we sent back over a hundred prisoners and killed and wounded many more. Perhaps too little has been said about this night advance, for in the early stages there was little opposition but it gained a large piece of ground purely by surprise and anyone who has taken part in a night approach to contact will know the terrific strain imposed by this type of operation.

We prayed that the powers that be would let us fight by day in future but our prayers were unanswered and on the night of the 10th we were ordered to continue the advance southwards, crossing the main THURY HARCOURT road, down the unrecconnoitred and trackless side of a gorge-like valley and form a base by the little riverlet at the bottom. Whilst 2 SWB were attacking across the same little river but over to our left, 2 GLOSTERS were going for THURY HARCOURT itself, well on our

17

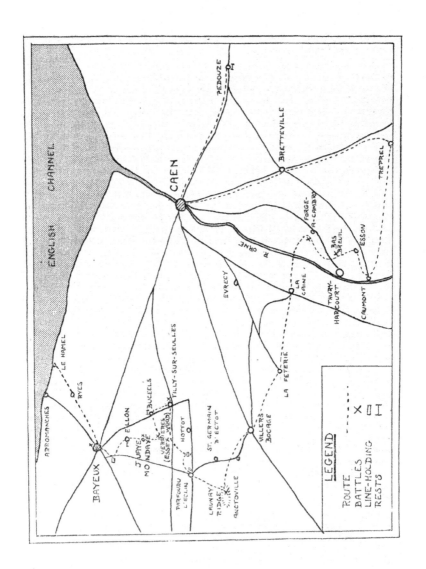

18

right flank. Returning to our own plan, it was the intention to pass two other platoons initially through the firm base, up the steep densely wooded slopes beyond and to secure additional firm bases in the BAS BREUIL WOOD before the rest of the Battalion went over to consolidate the high ground overlooking the villages of ESSON and CAUMONT-SUR-ORNE.

Once more we set out at last light with "A" Company leading and just a shade of moonlight helped us to find our way. Silence was imperative but as we clambered down the steep sides of the valley it became virtually impossible to avoid making noise. So dense were the trees that the night became pitch black and it was necessary for each man to hang on to the fellow in front and everytime somebody fell his weapon or equipment would clatter on the rocky ground and all the other weapons in the platoon would jangle against their neighbours and everybody would giggle like school kids and admonish the men in front and behind to be more quiet. It seemed hours before we reached the river and when we finally did arrive, we found the Boche in possession but sublimely innocent of our approach. We waited awhile and listened to the sentries talking and heard some of their horse transport moving on the far side. 8 Platoon wormed their way forward and so surprised the Boche that a few shots left us in possession of the stepping-stones that were the only crossing, though the water was only inches deep. Immediately 9 and 7 Platoons in that order were passed through and they vanished into the jungle beyond — for that was all it could be called. Dawn found them still searching for the tracks that appeared on the map and in the gathering light the job became easier and by 0600 hours both platoons reported in position; 9 Platoon in the centre of BAS BREUIL controlling the maze of rides and 7 Platoon the southern edge overlooking the open country that ran down to ESSON.

In view of the total absence of any sort of passage for vehicles, it was impossible to carry out the original plan. Tac Bn. HQ was established by the river crossing and "B" Company sat with them guarding the approaches and enduring continuous shelling. The two leading platoons of "A" retained their hold on the wood supported by a dismounted section of Carriers whilst "C" Company were also across the river looking after the right flank and linking up with the forward Company. So we stayed all day and night in a most unenviable position and all the time the Boche sent our patrols to find out where we were and what we were doing. Mainly we left them alone as it suited our purpose but those that pried too closely had to be dealt with. Early next morning 7 Platoon were attacked by three strong fighting patrols and, hopelessly outnumbered and outgunned, they pulled back and joined up with 9 Platoon. Here both platoons were surrounded and cut off and the area sprayed with small arms from all angles. Sjt. Skittrall makes another contribution to the story here, as oblivious to danger, he walked upright down the track leading into the Boche positions. A flood of bullets greeted him but he reached one of our wounded, leisurely picked him up and brought him in to his own positions and then carried him through the enemy cordon to the SBs before returning with badly needed ammunition.

At 1600 hrs. in the afternoon a strong attack developed against "C" Company from the right flank, 13 Platoon was overrun and bloody hand-to-hand fighting took place around Company HQ, during which Captain P. Chell was killed with many of his men. Always the attacker could approach to within a few yards before being detected in the dense undergrowth, but somehow the positions were maintained, though one remembers marked maps and secret codes being burnt "just in case". All communications had now gone, but the CO read the battle by sound and directed three regiments of 25-pounders and some 4.2" mortars on the enemy. Many of the shells bursting in the trees caused casualties to our own fellows, but it was nothing compared to the damage done to the attackers. Gradually the attack and the artillery dwindled and once more the positions were adjusted though never relinquished. How well one remembers L/Cpl. Jeffs walking alone up to advanced platoons with a message from HQ, and his remark when he found the positions intact: "Blimey, we thought you were all dead. You can come back now". "D" Coy. now took over in the wood, with "A" Company on the high ground to the left, and the remnants of "C" Company down by the river. Apart from some vicious "Nebelwerfering" the night was reasonably quiet, and we even slept a little.

On the 13th 2 GLOSTERS took THURY HARCOURT and we advanced through the BAS BREUIL WOOD over the already putrified dead Germans and found the enemy pulling out in a panic. In the burning and shell shattered village of ESSON we found hundreds of Tellermines hurriedly and amateurishly spread over all the roads. The Pioneer Platoon removed scores, but many were dealt with by the Rifle Coys. removing detonators as they pushed through the village still inhabited by the French. Inevitably all the mines were not removed, and casualties were suffered as vehicles went up. Swinging right-handed we approached the ORNE once more and plans were made should the enemy still be holding the line of steep hills running South-East from CAUMONT. But the enemy had gone and we met only a Battalion of the SOUTH STAFFS, who had just forced another crossing of the ORNE in this area. In this beautiful spot we stayed for two days, bathing in the lovely river and being welcomed by the civilians who had remained through all. Contact with the enemy was completely lost, and it was even said that there were no Boche within twenty miles.

17 August found us at TREPREL near FALAISE and, being in reserve, we were not really in at the kill of the German 7th Army at the famous FALAISE GAP Indeed the only real incident was the bombing by a Boche intruder aircraft of some ammunition trucks and the exploding shells, mortar bombs and small arms, kept us from our badly needed sleep. With the disbanding of 59 Div., 56 Bde. replaced another Bde. in 49 (WR) Inf. Div. and so we left 30 Corps and came under command of 1 British Corps in Canadian Army. We assumed our new position on the 19th and moved to a little place called PEDOUZE, famous to us only for its mosquitoes which appeared to be the size of Messerschmitts, and dysentery entry.

WITH THE POLAR BEARS TO LE HAVRE

With all the Anglo-American front sweeping forward, we patted one another on the back and decided we should never catch up with the Boche again. We even made our plans for the victory celebrations which surely could not be very long delayed. Thus it was rude shock when the afternoon of 24 August found us outside the town of CORMEILLES, with the Germans still inside. CORMEILLES is a pretty little town, set in some beautiful wooded country, with numbers of small streams and rivers winding through the valleys. Little need be written about this attack for, compared with past experiences, it was a milk-and-water affair with almost no fighting. Again a dusk attack was planned and men from the FFI were allotted to each of the leading Companies as local guides. "B Coy. led off and quickly seized the Western half of the town, straddling a river, the bridge over which had been blown by the departing enemy. Losing no time, "A" Coy. passed through and as they entered the main square, the remaining Boche fled from the far side and the civilians appeared in a flash with white flags and Cognac. "C" Coy. consolidated on the high ground to the East and North-East and the place was secure, with patrols pushing out in all directions. The 25th was a gala day in CORMEILLES with everything free for the British. Champagnes and wines were unearthed from where they had been hidden from the Boche, and in return it was the old story of "cigarette pour 'Papa" and "chocolat pour BéBé". We met several RAF types in CORMEILLES. Dressed in blue overalls, clogs and little French berets, they came up to us and as we prepared to "parler Francais", were dumbfounded when they would say "Christ, I thought you blokes were never coming!" Shot down in raids over France, they had escaped and gone into hiding, coming out only at night to work with the Maquis.

On 26 August the Battalion was once more moving eastward and the early afternoon found us only a mile from PONT AUDEMER, a fair sized town situated on both sides of the LA RISLE River, which, running North, empties into the SEINE opposite LE HAVRE. Men from 6 Airborne Div. had a precarious hold on the western half of the town. All the bridges were blown and on the eastern side of the river the enemy were firmly entrenched, with 88s and MGs emplaced in the buildings covering all approaches and possible crossing places. It was vitally necessary to force the river so that bridges could be built enabling men and materials to take the shortest route to the East in an effort to liquidate the remains of the German Army still on our side of the SEINE. The first attempt was made rather more than a mile to the South, but the noise of the assault boats being launched gave the show away and the river was swept with Spandau fire and the area lit up with Verey lights. A number of casualties were suffered and the project abandoned as further movement became impossible. A secondary effort was then made in the town centre. The site of the main bridge was chosen and an hour before dawn elements of "A" Coy. slid down the steep banks and waded waist deep acroos the swiftly flowing river amongst the masses of débris. One section made the crossing undetected and took up positions in buildings on the far bank but the second section were only half way over phen Boche sentry woke up and threw a number of grenades amongst the wading troops. This was the signal for all the 88s and spandaus to open up and the whole area was sprayed with crossfire making further movement impossible. At dawn the position was that we held a couple of wrecked buldings on the far bank completely encircled by Germans who unsuccessfully asked us to surrender. This stalemate continued till the early afternoon with intermittent shelling and sniping when, secretly, the Boche began to pull out, threatened by encirclement from a British force moving northwards

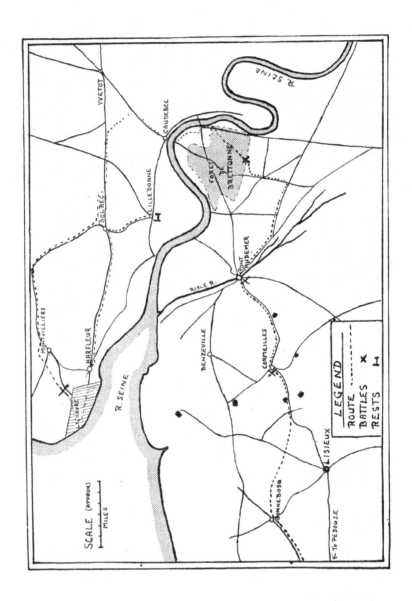

SCALE (APPROX)
MILES

R. SEINE

R. SEINE

LEGEND
ROUTE
BATTLES ✕
RESTS ⊢

YVETOT
CAUDEBEC
BOLBEC
LILLEBONNE
FÔRET DE BRETTONNE
MONTIVILLIERS
HARFLEUR
LE HAVRE
BENZEVILLE
CORNEILLES
PONT AUDEMER
RISLE R.
LISIEUX
BONNEBOSQ
←TO PEDOUZE

on the enemy side of the river. Cautiously dashing from house to house we found the enemy gone and at 1500 hrs. the rest of the Battalion crossed and Sappers began work on the bridge.

On the 28th we reached the South Western edge of the FORET-DE-BRETONNE, a large wooded area running right down to the SEINE. This was the only area still remaining in German hands and it contained masses of material of all kinds, thousands and thousands of horses and a few thousand Germans who had missed the last ferry and were waiting to be evacuated by raft under cover of night. Limited attacks on the 29th found the area heavily mined and spandaus, covering all approaches, caused many casualties. On the following day with 2 SWB encircling the wood from the left, we began to drive straight through the centre spraying the rides and undergrowth with automatics as we went and lifting Tellermines by the score. We took many prisoners and drove many more into the hands of 2 SWB who had got round the back. By mid afternonn the pocket was finished and the cages full of PW. The FORET-DE-BRETONNE proved to be what everybody had hoped — the graveyard of the bulk of the equipment of the 7th Army. Everything was there that goes to make an Army, but most of all we appreciated the horses that gave us two days of riding, as almost every man acquired his own mount.

We stayed in the area of CAVAUMONT and LA MAILLERAYE for two more days and on 2 September the Battalion crossed the SEINE by raft, assault boats and all kinds of amphibious craft. Whilst the British Army were going flat out for BELGIUM and the bulk of the Canadian Army was directed on to the PAS-DE-CALAIS area, 49 Div. were ordered to take LE HAVRE, assisted by 51st Div. when the latter had sorted out St. VALERY and FECAMP. So, having crossed the SEINE, we swung westwards and concentrated near the village of ALLIQUERVILLE. All available troop transport was being used elsewhere but fortunately a few heavy German Diesel vehicles had been "acquired" and these slightly assisted in the ferrying of the Battalion over such a long distance. On 3 Sept. we took over from 49 Recce Regt. at LE MESNIL and flanked by other Battalions we "contained" the Boche in LE HAVRE. The enemy had withdrawn most of his outposts into the main perimeter defences and mighty strong these were. MONTIVILLIERS had been abandoned and this town was in the hands of the Maquis and a platoon of "B" Coy. The river LEZARDE had been dammed and large areas of surrounding country flooded and made impassable. We were relieved by 11 RSF on the 5 th and moved round to the North near the little village of LE TOT and close to FONTENAY. The next four days were spent patrolling to the German defence belt, recconnoitering routes and studying air photos and defence overprints. Masses of information came to us from the FFI, a lot of it useful, much inaccurate. As usual the force inside the port was under-estimated. We worked on a German Strenghth of 5—7000 and actually took over 11,000 prisoners.

Operation "ASTONIA" which was the code name given to the plan for the capture of LE HAVRE, was scheduled to begin on 9 Sept. but torrential rain which turned the country into a sea of mud caused a 24-hr. postponement and the attack did not start until the evening of the 10th. In the days preceeding, Bomber Command systematically pulverised all

LE HAVRE "His foes are so enrooted with his friends
That, plucking to unfix an enemy,
He doth unfasten so and shake a friend."

the known strongpoints and to the RAF must go much of the credit for
the amazing success of the attack. The bigger plan for the assault was
that 56 Bde. should capture the strong points in the FONTAINE-LE-
MALLET area and seize the bridges spanning the LEZĀRDE river which
ran at right angles from the FORET-DE-MONTGEON. 146 and 147 Bdes.
would then push through and exploit inside the main defence belt whilst
51 (H) Div. passed through our right flank and drove for the sea South
of OCTEVILLE, thus getting behind the main defences on their sector. The
final phase comprised the drives of 49 Div. westward to the sea and 51
Div. southward to the 29 Grid Line.

The weather improved on the 10 th and in the late afternoon we
watched Lancasters and Halifaxes putting the finishing touches to the
obliteration of the defences. As twilight fell, searchlights came on and
gave us first experience of artificial moonlight aiding a night attack. Off
went the Flails to breach the minefields and the AVREs followed to bridge
the anti-tank ditches and blast open the concrete pill boxes. Then came
2 SWB and 2 GLOSTERS to secure the initial eight strongpoints and behind
followed 2 ESSEX mounted on armoured troop-carrying Kangaroos. As
we moved up behind the leading Battalions reports of objectives taken
came back over the air with heartening regularity. Despite all difficulties,

24

2 GLOSTERS did not pause until their effort was completed, but 2 SWB had a much harder fight and suffered heavy casualties before capturing their final strongpoint. As our turn came, the troops left their Kangaroos and quickly mopped up all 2 ESSEX objectives before pushing patrols over the bridges on to the high ground beyond. Our own casualties totalled only 8 wounded for the scores of prisoners we took and the mass of booty we acquired.

There was very little fight left in the Boche and as day dawned and other brigades passed through, the dozens of prisoners swelled into hundreds and on 12 September when we took our place in the race for the sea, the prisoners were being counted in bundles of a thousand. Civilians came running into the streets to tell us where the Germans were hiding and off would go a section of men to return with ten times their number of prisoners. One diminutive Essex man was found marching alone at the head of a long column of fully armed Boche, when asked what the score was, replied "50". As we gently pointed out that there were over 200 Germans in the party he said "Well Guv, there was only 50 of the — —s there when I started !!" If you are interested in figures, 49 Div. alone took 8000 prisoners of which 2900 were claimed by 56 Bde. Total British casualties amounted to 400 all ranks killed and wounded. So was LE HAVRE captured and a great port made available for shipping. The SEINE was open all the way to PARIS and our supply problem solved with an ease most unexpected.

We stayed only one more night in LE HAVRE, which was a great pity, as there were untold stocks of all kinds of wines and spirits in the German stores and most of it had to be left for the fellows who had not fought for it. However when we moved into LILLEBONNE on the following day, we did not go quite empty handed and even now, maybe, someone still has a bottle or so of Champagne or Suze "Réservé á Wehrmacht".

THROUGH FRANCE AND BELGIUM TO RYCKEVORSEL.

Five whole days we rested at LILLEBONNE, a pretty little town in wooded Seine valley country and there we slept and refitted and were reinforced. "D" Coy., which had been disbanded through casualties and lack of replacements, was reformed into a training Company, and after our fill of sleep we all did a little gentle training. We even found a football and played the local side. Perhaps someone still still keeps one of the French posters as a souvenir and laughs over the heading "La LILLEBONNAISE versus THE ESSEX REGIMENT and his professional players". We were all sorry when, on 18 Sept., we left to continue our period of peace at AVESNES-EN-VAL only a dozen miles from DIEPPE. AVESNES was little more than a cluster of country houses but for all that it was a pleasant little place, almost untouched by war and most suited to ensure a rest after the celebrations in LILLEBONNE.

By the third week in September BRUSSELS and most of ANTWERP were in British hands and so, when we left AVESNES on the 22nd, we had a long two-day drive to catch up with the fighting. It was a drive we shall

25

LIST OF AWARDS

DISTINGUISHED SERVICE ORDER

Lt. Col. M. A. H. Butler, M. C.

MEMBER OF THE ORDER
OF THE BRITISH EMPIRE

Capt. J. Townrow

MILITARY CROSS

Major D. W. Browne
Major M. W. Holme
Major P. J. Wilkins
The Rev. W. R. Thomas
Captain D. J. Selvage
Captain W. F. MacMichael, M. C. (Bar to M. C.)
Lieut. M. Leavey
Lieut. J. Cooper
Lieut. J. N. Orr
Lieut. R. B. Sellors
Lieut. R. G. Filby
Lieut. H. A. S. Cooper

DISTINGUISHED CONDUCT MEDAL

Cpl. B. J. Shaw
Cpl. W. Skittrall

MILITARY MEDAL

L/Cpl. W. Worwood
Pte. J. Giles
Cpl. C. Sturman
Cpl. W. Coe
Cpl. H. Whitehall
Pte. J. Jordan
CSM. A. Morgan
Pte. F. Holland
Cpl. I. W. Walters
Cpl. F. Bucknell

CROIX DE GUERRE WITH VERMILION STAR

Lieut. R. G. Filby

CROIX DE GUERRE WITH BRONZE STAR

Cpl. W. Skittrall

MENTIONED IN DESPATCHES

Major P. R. Barrass
Major M. W. Holme
Lieut. R. G. Filby
Lieut. A. A. Vince
Cpl. H. C. Sizzey
Cpl. F. Tyrrell
Pte. W. Burt
Cpl. W. Skittrall
Sgt. E. Stothert
Cpl. G. Danby

COMMANDER-IN-CHIEF'S CERTIFICATE

Capt. W. J. Barry
RSM. J. R. Gulliver
CSM. V. E. Wood
Sgt. J. Pullen
Sgt. H. Conn
Cpl. C. Inman
L/Cpl. R. Jeffs
Sgt. F. Mayes
Sgt. G. A. Smith
Sgt. L. Andrews
Sgt. A. Slammers
Sgt. W. Crabb

never forget. For over two hundred miles the route was lined with cheering, flag — waving French and Belgians who showered us with fruit, flowers, wine and everything they could spare. And was it purely by coincidence that we stopped the night of the 22nd at PHALEMPIN, near CARVIN, where many of us had happy memories of the days before the DUNKIRK evacuation? Certainly the billets appeared very empty after the evening meal had finished.

The night of the 23rd. found us at HELLEBURG, near LIERRE, and we stayed there until the 25th when we moved up to OOSTMALLE in preparation for the relief of a Battalion of the KOYLI who were having a sticky time battling in the outskirts of RYCKEVORSEL. The Boche were now trying to hold the line of the ANTWERP-TURNHOUT CANAL and a heavy price had already been paid for the limited bridgehead obtained. The KOYLI were the most forward of our troops and, as we have said, they held the southern part of RYCKEVORSEL with the Boche still firmly holding the town itself. We moved up in the evening, but desultory fighting and much shelling was still taking place and the take-over was postponed till dark. Relief was complete well before dawn and "A", "B" and "C" Coys. all improved their positions. In the centre contact was from house to house, but on the the flanks "A" and "B" Coys. had better fields of fire across meadow land.

The enemy launched limited attacks during the day, the heaviest being on our right, but we continued to improve our positions and bagged fifty prisoners. Shelling was heavy on both sides and casualties frequent. Activity flared up at dawn on the 27th with a large enemy barrage and smoke screen. The CO brought up two troops of Canadian Shermans from reserve to thicken up the defence but the expected attack was pressed home and both "A" and "B" Coys., who bore the brunt, were presented with a perfect target when the attacking infantry came out of the smoke screen. The Boche threw in six companies totalling over 500 men, but all to no avail. 12 Platoon of "B" Coy. were temporarily cut off but contact re-established almost as their ammunition was exhausted. Both the leading Coys. took a tremendous toll in killed and wounded as they mowed down Boche at point blank range. Over 100 enemy dead were counted on the battlefield and many prisoners taken. This proved to be their final effort and, seizing the initiative, the CO ordered "B" and "C" Coys. to secure the remaining half of the town. Only mortars and artillery interfered with this operation, though once again casualties were numerous. RYCKEVORSEL was only a small battle and probably it does not appear in the history books, but it was one of our better efforts. Control was perfect on all levels despite the terrible job the Signals had in in keeping the lines repaired. Every objective was taken as directed and the men behind the rifles and Brens rarely wasted a bullet. Our own casualties are not available, maybe around the 60 mark, but if an estimate of 400 is given as the German losses, it will be realised that this is a conservative figure when one recalls the 200 prisoners and the hundred-plus bodies counted. The Battalion received several decorations for this action, none more deserved than the MM awarded to CSM Morgan of "B" Coy.

On 1 October we sadly said goodbye to Lt. Col. G. G. Elliott as he left us for another job. This story will only be doing its bare duty if we say that we would ask for no better Commanding Officer. The Special Order of the Day in which he said goodbye to his men is reproduced herewith.

SPECIAL ORDER OF THE DAY.
By Lt. Col. G. G. Elliott.

Today I am leaving you to go to another job in Middle East. This note is to say goodbye to you all, as there is no·time or opportunity to see you personally.

You and I have travelled a long and difficult road together, starting on the beaches on D Day, passing through BAYEUX, TILLY and countless other places which you and I will never forget.

We have had many successes. We have our difficult times too. But whatever the difficulties and however hard the tasks, you have never failed to do your duty and do your share.

I have been very proud of you and I shall always be very proud too that I have had the honour of commanding such a fine Battalion.

I know you will accord my successor the same loyal support you have always given me.

For the war is not over yet and you still have to get to the end of the road on which we started together on D Day. I shall be watching your progress along that road and always regretting that I shall not be with you at the finish.

Goodbye , God bless you and Good luck to you all.

(sd) G. G. Elliott.

1 Oct. 44. Lt. Col.

Under the new CO Lt. Col. N. W. Finlinson D. S. O., the Battalion held the line at RYCKEVORSEL until the morning of 7 October. Almost ten days of continuous deep patrolling and under constant shellfire. The enemy once more kept changing his positions and several patrols had casualties where previous sorties had made no contact. So thinly were we spread over the ground that "S" Coy., in addition to their normal commitments with the Rifle Coys., formed a composite force to hold part of the line, flanked with another force made up from the MT. But on this sector all idea of attack had passed from the Wehrmacht and from now on they devoted themselves almost exclusively to delaying actions.

ACTIONS ON THE DUTCH-BELGIAN BORDER.

On 7 October we were relieved by a composite group known as BOBFORCE, comprised of LAA Regts. and A/Tank Regts. fighting as infantry. That night the Battalion dug in near the small town of POPPEL where the rest of 49 Div. had been scrapping and we were told that our next job was Holland, with the town of TILBURG as our particular objective. However, on the 9th, plans were changed once more; the new order was defence, and the whole of this sector became static. On the

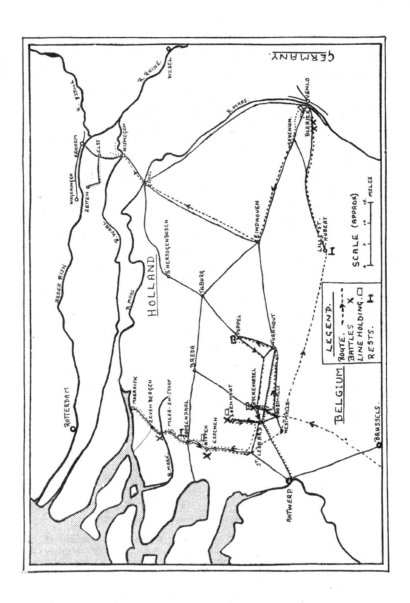

13th "D" Coy. was reconstituted and we were back to four Rifle Coys. again. We held the line North of POPPEL for 10 days. 10 days of rain, with slit trenches ankle deep in water and mud, and the Boche only a few hundred yards away and movement by day impossible. The endless patrols and shelling and mortaring did little to cheer us up, and it began to seem as if the end of the war was as remote as ever.

However, the period of waiting came to the end and, after being relieved by an infantry Battalion of the Polish Armoured Division, we concentrated on the 19th in the small town of St. LEONARDS. A little to the West of RYCKEVORSEL 49 Div. were attacking northwards in conjunction with 3 Canadian Infantry Div. on the left flank and, still further to the left, mixed forces of British and Canadians were clearing the SCHELDT ESTUARY and the islands of WALCHEREN and North and South BEVELAND. The big idea, of course, being to open the SCHELDT to our shipping and enable supplies to be landed at ANTWERP. In front of us the enemy were firmly dug in on marshy ground favouring the defence and they were well supported by artillery and SP guns. As far as the ESSEX were concerned, the Boche held a line in depth a couple of miles South of the small town of LOENHOUT, with their forward positions a similar distance North of us. We were directed on to LOENHOUT whilst 2 GLOSTERS attacked on our right and 2 SWB were ordered to put in "worrying" efforts from their base at BRECHT towards BEEKHOVEN. Once again a direct frontal assault was ordered and in view of the strength of the enemy defences we were allotted considerable support.

Surprise and firepower provided the keystone for the success of the attack. At 0728 hrs. on 20 October, four Regiments of 25-pounders, three Regiments of 5.5s and all available 3" and 4.2" mortars commenced a detailed fire programme on the Boche positions and, two minutes later, Tanks, Crocodiles and Infantry crossed the taped start line. "B" Coy. took only thirteen minutes to secure their initial objectives but "C" on the left ran into very strong enemy positions in the little village of STAPELHEIDE which had been little affected by the artilery concentrations. Every hedgerow was honeycombed with well built weapon pits, all inter-communicating, and for eight hours "C" Coy fought from ditch to ditch supported by flamethrowers and tanks before they could report over the air that all their objectives had been captured. This Coy. bore almost all our casualties for the entire action. Five killed and many wounded and a complete troop of tanks knocked out did STAPELHEIDE cost. Whilst "C" Coy. were still fighting their battle, Lt. Col. Finlinson D. S. O. ordered up "A" Coy. to join "B" Coy. and continue the advance in the centre. With tank support both these Coys. drove forward and, as darkness fell, they were holding the South Eastern portion of LOENHOUT with only disorganised remnants of the enemy in the rest of the town. 2 ESSEX took over three hundred prisoners that day, though, as we have indicated, the cost to us of this four mile advance was not light. The final liberation of the town was completed next morning when, at first light, our carriers and tanks drove right through with the Rifle Coys, house clearing in the rear. Forty five more prisoners were collected in this operation and another successful battle added to the growing list.

29

RYCKEVORSEL "For all the soil of the achievement goes,
With me, into the earth."

Funny people are the inhabitants of LOENHOUT. With much of the
town shattered by shellfire and most of the surrounding farms razed to the
ground by the fleeing Boche, they came complaining that, in addition to
liberating the town, we had whipped a couple of typewriters. As if the
infantryman wants to add a typewriter to the weight of a PIAT or a Bren
as he plods from BAYEUX to BERLIN!! Two more days we stayed in
LOENHOUT enduring some healthy hostile shelling, whilst on the left the
Boches threw in several desperate counter-attacks in an attempt to halt
this already considerable advance.

You have probably read in the press stories about 104 US Inf. Div.
(The Timberwolves) when they took part in the savage ARDENNES
fighting in January 1945. Their first introduction to the line came when
they relieved us at LOENHOUT on 23 October and they were very anxious
to learn all the tricks from such old hands as ourselves. Unfortunately
we heard later they found out the answers the hard way. After a night
in ST. LEONARDS, we took over positions from an infantry battalion of
4 Canadian Armoured Div. a few hundred yards south of the small town
of ESSCHEN. ESSCHEN is a long straggly town astride the Dutch-
Belgian border and, as near as makes no difference, the border was the
dividing line between ourselves and the enemy. Obviously the Canadians
had been fighting very hard, for such of ESSCHEN as we held was badly
knocked about and heavy shelling on both sides was still proceeding. Il
is difficult now to compare the shelling from one battle to another but

30

we mainly agree that seldom was more dirt slung at us than when we operated around ESSCHEN and NISPEN. The Boche had many excellent OPs and only a small amount of movement on our part brought forth an immediate and heavy concentration of shells, mostly 88s and 150s.

The attack on NISPEN was another hurried affair and we had little time to recce and no time at all to patrol. However, the lines of approach to our start line were taped in the darkness of 25/26 October and we formed up at first light for the attack on the broken country West of the village. Once having captured our objective and cut off the enemy's retreat, 2 GLOSTERS had the task of clearing NISPEN itself. The barrage opened at 0630 hrs. and thirty minutes later, "A" Coy. on the right and "B" Coy. on the left, crossed the start line supported by Tanks and Crocodiles of 9 ROYAL TANK REGIMENT and 1 FIFE & FORFARSHIRE YEOMANRY respectively. The attack was not made any easier when we found that the Battalion which should have secured our start line had been unable to flush a large wood immediately in front and consequently the leading Coys. had a minor battle which had not appeared on the programme. The Tanks, Crocs. and Infantry all fought magnificently and by 0834 hrs. both Companies had completed the 2000 yards advance and were quickly digging slits in face of colossal enemy retaliatory shelling. "D" Coy., in an effort to cut off the enemy in NISPEN, drove through "A" Coy. for the road bridge over the canal North of the village, but ran into heavy small arms and 88mm fire as they traversed the open ground in front of the primary objective. Most of 17 Platoon became casualties and both the remaining Infantry and the tank crews did wonderful work evacuating the wounded under short range small arms fire.

Once more our tally of prisoners taken reached the three figure mark and altogether that morning we sent back 106 representatives of the "Master Race". We look back on the battle of NISPEN not only as another victory, but as a perfect example of infantry-tank cooperation. When we parted a day or so later, we said goodbye to what we thought must be quite the pick of the black hats, and maybe they thought as kindly of us. For the rest of that day we endured tremendous shelling which ploughed up the whole of the Battalion area. As usual every Coy. decided that they were the only targets, whilst Bn. HQ was quite certain that every shell was directed at the Command Post. However, as day turned into night and night into day, the barrage began to dwindle as the Boche pulled back their guns to avoid losing them, for Shelreps came flooding in to enable our own gunners to pinpoint the enemy artillery and take counter-battery action.

As October drew to a close the Boche continued to retreat on the MAAS and, with other units, we achieved a bloodless occupation of ROOSENDAAL, a large rail and manufacturing town little more than ten miles from the estuary of that great river which has become famous in so many wars. Nevertheless, a few actions still remained to be fought before this portion of the campaign in Southern HOLLAND can be dismissed. We had just three days at ROOSENDAAL in billets which we occupied on two further occasions and there most of us, for the second time in the campaign, experienced civilian society as the inhabitants gave us the freedom of their homes. The enemy were now holding grimly to the line of the river MARK, which runs approximately from West to East halfway between ROOSENDAAL and the MAAS and, on the northern side of the river, the Boche were holding such towns and riverpoints as WILLEMSTAD, MOERDIJK and GEERTRUIDENBERG. So that the already extended Canadian line could be more easily held, 49 Div. were ordered to force the MARK and clear the enemy from the pocket South of the MAAS. 2 ESSEX were allotted the task crossing the MARK silently by night just South of the little village of BARLAQUE, whilst an American Combat Team performed a similiar operation on our right but with all the noise of artillery preparation and support laid on.

The Germans still had a small bridgehead at STAMPERSGAT on our side of the river and, at 2030 hrs. on 2 November, 2 GLOSTERS began their attempt to iron this pocket out. Simultaneously 104 US Div. commenced their effort at STANDDAARBUITEN and we crossed our own start line. "A" Coy. provided the boat-carrying, launching and local protection parties and at 2100 hrs. they reported by wireless that everything was ready. So far opposition had been non-existent but much of the DF put down by the Boche against the Yanks was falling unpleasantly close to us and the whole area was being sprayed by MGs. This was particularly unpleasant as all the fields had been flooded by the Boche and we had to stick to one main built up road for the first mile and then move along a single track already ankle deep in mud and rapidly deteriorating. "C" Coy. moved up immediately on receipt of "A" Coy.'s message and commenced to cross, a section at a time, in each of two assault boats. Already line was working from the crossing point back through ferry control to Bn. HQ and, all through that never-ending night, the line was kept working. Shells tore it to shreds but never was the line communication out for more than a few minutes as several Signal parties patrolled and repaired the whole length. Unfortounately "C" Coy. were unable to complete their crossing before being discovered and the Boche brought down all his artillery and mortars on the crossing point and line of approach. Casualties began to mount but "A" Coy. continued to pull in the loaded boats to the far bank and pull them back again empty. "C' Coy., having finished crossing, pushed inland and found BARLAQUE empty, and then swung right-handed to seize an important bridge over a canal, during which operation they took a number of prisoners, whilst an assault section of Pioneers "deloused" the bridge which had been prepared for blowing.

"C" were now firmly on all their objectives but "B" and "D", who followed in that order, had little success in their attacks to the North against the village of KADE and to the West, parallel to the North bank of the river. In the early hours of the 3rd, the A/Tank Platoon ferried two 6-pounder guns and towing Jeep across the river and this magnificent effort did much to ensure the final success of the operation. Shelling and mortaring continued on a big scale and, shortly after dawn, the Boche put in several attacks in an effort to rub out the bridgehead. These met with some initial success and both "B" and "D" Coys. had a bad time on the left. Here it was that the "S" Coy. detachment manning the forward A/Tank gun, almost entirely unaided, took on numbers far

PANTHER TANK "She is pistol proof, Sir,
You shall hardly offend her."

greater than their own and never gave in inch of ground in the face of the most resolute attacks. On the right, "C" Coy. were solid as rock and gradually the position swung in our favour as the enemy faltered and eventually withdrew, leaving many dead and wounded on the roads and in the ditches. With the final success of the 2 GLOSTERS and the completion of a class 40 bridge, the battle was largely over, but another 24 hours passed before we were relieved and returned to ROOSENDAAL to dry out and rest. In the bigger picture, the forcing of the river MARK occupies only a minor part, but those who were there will forever remember the bleak, desolate and flooded country, the single, shell-swept track with the only cover a mound of turnips, the cattle that died as they swam for a little bit of dry land and the bullets that plopped in the water seemingly as harmless as peas from a pea-shooter.

After six weeks in the line almost without a break we had been promised a rest but, on 6 November, the Battalion was again at short notice and on the following day we took over from 414 Regimental Combat Team of 104 US Div. just outside MOERDIJK. This river port was one of the two remaining pockets South of the MAAS, and a most unpleasant place it was. With flooded fields and wrecked farm houses, one could only live in the banks beside the roads, and the roads were regularly shelled by heavy guns from the North bank. However, we only played a very minor role in this little affair and our operational activity was

33

confined to "containing" and patrols, whilst the Polish Armoured Div. attacked from the South East. The enemy did not last very much longer in MOERDIJK and on the 9th we were back in ROOSENDAAL for the last time.

Six days we stayed in ROOSENDAAL, resting, training, drilling and playing football. There is little the average infantryman enjoys more than to come out of the line after weeks and months of hard battles and then to get cracking on some drill and weapon training. However, somebody told us to do it and so, rather than start an argument, we did it and looked as if we liked it. About this time short leave started and the lucky few went off to GHENT, BRUSSELS or ANTWERP for 48 hrs. of complete freedom. Mainly they needed a complete rest when they returned but, more than anything, this privilege cheered us up and provided something for which to look forward.

On 15 November 49 Div. temporarily severed connections with the Canadian Army and came under command 12 Corps in the British 2nd. Army. The same day we left ROOSENDAAL for the last time, but even now if you go back, your ESSEX shoulder titles will bring crowds of the inhabitants into the streets, wanting to know how Tom, Dick and Harry are and you will not go short of a bed and what food they can spare. It is well to remember that when the old "bowler hat" is firmly planted on the head we can still do a great service to International Relations by revisiting the places we helped to liberate and where we were so well received — though maybe it will be necessary for the few to be discreet if they go accompanied by their wives or girl friends. The departure on the 15 th began a succession of moves eastwards during which we paused at the small towns of LILLE-ST-HUBERT and WEERT before fetching up at PANNINGEN in the evening of the 21st. It was at LILLE-ST-HUBERT that we rather blotted our copy-book when the female owner of the house where we had a small Officers Mess, took exception to a convivial band of officers playing "Hi-Cock-Alorum" in her lounge. One can well understand the doubts anyone would feel about the foundations of a house with Major MacMichael leaping around, but secretly we decided that the female was a collaborator and had we not departed early next day we should probably have called in the Field security chaps to check up on her. The funniest part of the incident was to see a lot of officers crawling meekly to bed like naughty school boys in the face of an irate mother.

With the approaching winter, the weather became very bad and the British Army was fighting only a limited action to clear the enemy from the western side of the river MEUSE in the general area of VENLO and ROERMOND. We took part in this for less than ten days and physical contact with the Boche was rare but nevertheless we won a considerable stretch of ground and sat at the wrong end of some very heavy shelling and mortaring. On 22 and 23 November the Battalion put in frontal attacks on the villages o'f KORTEHEIDE and LANGEHEIDE. In both efforts only limited artillery preparation was employed, for which we were very grateful as the Boche withdrew before us and the suffering of the civilians who remained was reduced to a minimum. We found mines everywhere and, as always, the Pioneer Platoon performed yeoman

34

service. Hostile artillery and mortar fire increased as we approached BLERICK and "B" Coy. particularly suffered very badly just outside LANGEHEIDE when, amidst a number of casualties, the Company Commander and Second-in-Command were both wounded. BLERICK is really a suburb of VENLO, with the former on the west bank of the MEUSE, joined to the main partof the town by road and rail bridges. The German frontier is very close to the river at this point and the Boche were holding the river line very strongly on the far bank and maintaining a fair sized force in BLERICK, behind which the bridges had not yet been blown.

On the 25th we were ordered to close in on the Boche and invest the town. A squadron of armoured troop-carrying vehicles called Kangaroos were allotted to the Battalion for the approach and in point of fact we were able to drive right on to our positions before dismounting. Possibly the Boche had previously decided not to hold the belt of woods around the town but to retire behind his masses of wire and Anti-Tank ditch. In any case, the only opposition as the Kangaroos smashed through the trees came from artillery and mortars which were mounted in great numbers on the East bank of the river. We sat outside BLERICK until we were relieved by the RECCE Regt. on 28 November and most of that time we had a company of 2 SWB under command, who were absolutely first-class. Enemy artillery remained very active and the shells bursting in the trees caused far more casualties than ground bursts would have done. However, every time the Boche shelled us our guns and mortars replied and, in one short period of a few hours on the 26th, the 3" mortars alone fired 1200 bombs. The Rifle Coys. patrolled the enemy defences without respite and a night never passed without two fighting patrols crossing the ditch, apart from more numerous reconnaissance efforts.

28 November 1944 was notable for two things. Firstly we left BLERICK and 2nd Army and, moving North once more, we reverted to the command of 1st Canadian Army. Secondly Lt. Col. M. A. H. Butler M. C. joined us and assumed command of the Battalion, a position he held until April 1945. He turned up in an old jeep-driver's coat which he kept losing on an average twice a week during his stay with us and, as the coat sported no badges of rank, very few of us knew who he was when he first arrived. Probably he did it on purpose so that he might, as he would have put it, "Have a Jimmy Dekko at the Prunes" without letting them put on their best behaviour for a new CO. Of course Lt. Col. Butler lost many other things beside his coat. Peter Butler bought him a "Utility" lighter once and he lost that every few hours and, when he found it, it would never work. His consumption of chinagraph pencils as he pored over maps was stupendous and his cigarette case was invariably empty. However, he never lost a battle, nor any of the large array of enemy weapons which stocked his personal armoury, until the Adjutant "whipped" his automatic rifle on the "Island".

THE ISLAND.

We have taken a long time running over our story but all our major efforts have been dealt with and now we come to the final Phase: a phase in which episodes such as VERRIERES, TILLY and the like will be missing and we have to recall the five months spent on and adjoining that water-logged piece of ground bounded by the rivers NEDER RIJN and WAAL and so aptly called "The Island". On the Southern edge of "The Island" lies the large town of NIJMEGEN, where 49 Div., by virtue of its long association with the place, gained the title of the "NIJMEGEN Home Guard". The bridges across the WAAL at NIJMEGEN had been captured intact by the 101 US Airborne Div. but, subsequently, a daring group of Boche had floated down river in "swimsuits" and blown lumps out and now two sections of Bailey spanned the gap in the road bridge and only a wire "catwalk" traversed the missing 100 yards of the rail bridge. A dozen miles to the North, on the far bank of the NEDER RIJN, is ARNHEM, forever guaranteed its place in History as the scene of the magnificent effort made by 1 British Airborne Div. to capture the RHINE crossings and make possible the breakthrough of the main British Army on to the Westphalian Plains of Germany. So well known is the story that no further reference to it is necessary here: suffice it to say that when we arrived on the "Island" on 1 Dec. 1945 the line had long since been stabilised. We took over from 6 DLI in the region of ELST, a badly shell-shattered town half way between ARNHEM and NIJMEGEN. Our left flank was in the hands of a Cameron Battalion of the 51 (H) Div. whose line swung Northwards, to reach the NEDER RIJN at HETEREN and

THE ISLAND "Let Heaven kiss Earth; now let not Nature's hand
Keep the wild Flood confined."

36

RANDWIJK. On our right was the balance of 49 Div. stretching down to the WAAL at HAALDEREN, leaving a large swampy stretch of ground including the villages of ELDEN, HUISSEN and ANGEREN to the enemy. Even before we came, the Boche had moved most of his artillery to the safe side of the NEDER RIJN, but there was still plenty of hostile shelling and mortaring and ELST itself, which had a couple of first class Church OPs, was the recipient of much "harrassing" fire in which 240mm guns often figured.

As we have already said, the Battalion was a long time on the "Island" and for long stretches we just sat tight in our built-up defences, for it was quite impossible to dig in, as water flooded in even as one removed the top spit. So it is not necessary and indeed it would be boring, to dwell too long on this final phase and we will content ourselves to cover the few major incidents and excitements that developed.

One such incident occurred almost before we had time to improve the defences to our particular liking. In the early afternoon of 2 December we heard an even louder than usual explosion and quickly everybody began to swot up "OPERATION NOAH". This was the apt title given to a huge sheaf of documents detailing moves to take place in the event of the Boche blowing the bund and allowing the waters of the NEDER RIJN to flood the "Island". "NOAH" never came into full operation, but the explosion we had heard was, in fact, the blowing of the bund South of ARNHEM and by midnight the flood waters were creeping up to our forward Coys. Gradually "A" and "C" Coys. were forced to give ground as the water gently rose and the Carrier platoon lined the Wetering canal to cover their withdrawal. In the early hours of the 3rd flooding increased more rapidly and both the forward Coys. were forced to swim out. All stores were got away in time apart from small quantities of ammunition and many head of cattle and poultry which sought refuge on little stretches of high (?) ground. The ammunition was salvaged by boat before dawn and the other items were "rescued" by boating patrols as and when they were needed. Thus do names like "Goose Farm" come back to our memory. As the water found its own level the rise became less apparent and we still held positions forward of ELST, where the flooding rarely rose above 18". On the left, the floods reached right down to the WAAL and 51 (H) Div. were forced back to the South of the Wetering canal, where they held strong points in villages such as VALBURG and ZETTEN, names which bring back many memories. The front was but little affected on the right and both the Boche and 49 Div. largely retained the original positions in the HAALDEREN-BEMMEL sector.

With a three mile stretch of "sea" in front and the bulk of the Battalion surrounded by water, our idea of transport had to be completely adjusted and we took to using DUKWS, amphibious Jeeps, Weasels and assault boats, both to get food up to the forward Coys. and, in many cases, for patrol work. For, with the advent of floods, patrolling had not ceased but had been intensified. The reason being, of course, that the line was very thinly held and it would have been the easiest job in the world for the Boche to have penetrated our isolated fortified houses. So snipers and patrols of varying strengths occupied the upper floors of flooded farm buildings well in front of our main defence line and gave us early warning of any enemy aggressive intentions. Patrol clashes were frequent and many "naval" engagements were fought in flimsy canvas assault boats, when victory mainly went to the side that fired first.

The Battalion was relieved on 14 Dec. and returned to its base at NIJMEGEN, where we had the minimum of time to clean up and get dried off before the majority of us had to go and guard a FMC in OSS: a job which we felt could have been done by some other types, to say the least of it.

We were not due back on the "Island" until Christmas Eve but, if you remember, it was around this time that the Boche began his large scale offensive in the ARDENNES and Monty was looking round for British Troops to help him reduce the salient that had been thrust into the American Line. 51 Div. on the "Island" was one of the formations he chose and thus it became necessary for 49 Div. to take over all their commitments and 2 ESSEX returned to the line on the 20th to take over from 5 CAMERONS in the VALBURG sector. Naturally the ground was now more thinly held than ever, with "A" Coy. under command of 2 GLOSTERS and occupying a very sticky position in ELST. The rest of the Battalion spent days building fire positions in upper rooms, laying mines and booby trapping unoccupied houses. Overhead, Flying Bombs

CAUSE " . . . should draw his several strengths together
And come against us in great puissance . . ."

38

soared on their way to LONDON and ANTWERP and often we could count up to a hundred a day. Reports of large concentrations of enemy Airborne forces directed against our sector caused no mean "flap" and most extensive precautions were taken, but as the days passed and the tide turned in the ARDENNES, the scare died away. The weather became intensely cold and, on Christmas Eve, a patrol of "B" Coy. which had boated almost up to the NEDER RIJN to observe the enemy, found themselves completely cut off by ice which was, as yet, insufficient to bear any great weight but still too thick to drive a boat through. Hope was almost abandoned, until a Weasel patrol found them half way home, hacking their way through the thickening ice with axes and rifle butts. Half frozen, tired and hungry, with the canvas boat shredded by ice floes, they had already made 2000 yards chest deep in water and ice, covering barely 100 yards an hour. Even that could not take the grin off their faces.

So life on the ARNHEM salient continued and days turned into weeks, weeks into months. Days and nights of ice and snow but with always the swiftly flowing currents where ice had only thinly formed. Such patches were the bugbear of patrols and this form of night entertainment, always a fearsome business, became even worse in these conditions. The reverberations of the creaking and cracking ice travelled miles and there was little future in being discovered inside the enemy lines with abso-

EFFECT " . . . he walked o'er perils, on an edge,
More likely to fall in than get o'er."

39

THE ISLAND " . . . and the wild dog
Shall flesh his tooth on every innocent."

lutely no cover at all. In one sector more than sixty fighting or recce
patrols were carried out in fourteen days and such was the standard of
patrol work that only the smallest casualties resulted. Many of the men
toured the Boche lines so often that they knew No Mans Land, the wire,
the mines and the enemy defence points almost as well as they did their
own.

The average tour of duty on the "Island" was four weeks in the line
and two weeks rest in NIJMEGEN, though the latter invariably incurred
irksome guard duties and reserve roles. Whilst we were enjoying one
such rest period, our band joined us and, although we were unable to see
them as much as we would have liked, Mr. Botting and his boys gave
us many a pleasant evening. It was during the same rest that the Boche
put in his attack on the villages of HEMMEN and ZETTEN and gave
us the oppotunity, in conjunction with 2 SWB, to win the battle of
ZETTEN.

ZETTEN was on the extreme left flank of the salient and when the
Boche attacked with brigade strength on 18 Jan. a Battalion   of   the
LEICESTERCHIRE Regt. was holding a very large area   including   the
village itself. The enemy met with fair initial success and recaptured
almost the whole of ZETTEN before the line was stabilised with the help
2 GLOSTERS. In the afternoon of the 19th, we were ordered   up   to

40

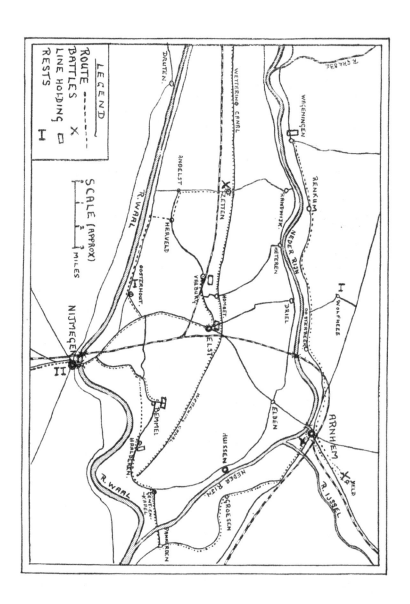

LEGEND

ROUTE ------
BATTLES X
LINE HOLDING ☐
RESTS I

SCALE (APPROX)
0 1 2 3 MILES

ZETTEN "Our men more perfect in the use of arms,
Our armour all as strong, our cause the better."

recapture all our original positions and throw the enemy back over the Wettering Canal. The attack was scheduled to go in at 0800 hrs on the 20th. but this flopped a little, for as we moved up in the darkness before dawn, knee deep in snow, we found that the Boche had infiltrated the defences in some strength and had created a strong point within 50 yards of where Bn. HQ had decided to operate. Here a dismounted Carrier Section had a tough fight and lost casualties before being taken prisoner in hopeless circumstances. Far from accepting the position, the section then proceeded to share its rations with the captors and gave the Boche a good heart-to-heart talk. It took nearly an hour, but our half dozen soldiers so convinced nearly thirty Boche of their own desperate plight that they agreed to becoming the captured instead of the captors. This episode by no mean relieved the general seriousness of the situation. "A" Coy. were brought up to pin the enemy and provide a firm base for the beginning of the major operation. Supported by a troop of 6 Canadian Armoured Regt., they so flooded the Boche with fire that "C" Coy, putting in a brilliant picture book right flanking attack, swept through the enemy positions with little opposition. Of the Germans, estimated to be a Company strong, who held this forward position, only one was known to have escaped. One Officer and twenty five ORs were taken prisoner and the balance killed or wounded.

42

ZETTEN "Come, we will all put forth, body and goods."

Reformed and again supported by Tanks, "A" Coy. then began the attack on ZETTEN itself. The War Correspondent, typing out his "front line" story in the depth of his BRUSSELS hotel, may have told you that the Boche in ZETTEN were poor troops, badly led and with little heart for the job of fighting. On the other hand, we shall tell you and we know that our sister Battalions will endorse what we say, that the enemy used very good class Para. boys and that mainly they fought with the utmost bravery, led by resolute officers and NCOs.; that in attack and defence their plans were good and their defence posts well sited and solidly built. "A" Coy. ran into the toughest opposition and fighting developed from house to house, room to room and then hand to hand. One Sherman Tank took twelve Bazooka hits and still kept firing its guns. The Company Commander was twice wounded and had to be evacuated and casualties began to reach serious proportions. "C" Coy. were now attacking on the left and meeting similar opposition. Neither side thought of quarter and slowly we forged ahead from one house to another, almost every room becoming a battlefield. One German Officer stood with his back to the wall in a passage, killing anyone who approached. Grenades were flung into the room, but he bore a charmed life until the Second-in-Command of "A" Coy. leapt into the passage and killed him with a bullet from his 38. A British NCO, throwing open a cellar door, found fourteen Boche waist deep in water and sprayed them with sten until they "jacked" in.

By 1330 hrs. in the afternoon, the two leading companies were in complete control of the centre of the village and little was left of the enemy. "D" Coy. then attacked the Northern half of ZETTEN and quickly secured all their objectives but suffered heavy casualties when their start line was plastered with mortars. The Company Commander was among the casualties. At first light next morning all the remaining houses and farm buildings were cleared, the 2 SWB completed the reduction of the KASTEEL area on our left and the few remaining Boche fled across the Wetering Canal to the little hamlet of INDOORNIK, which was immediately flattened by Typhoons, artillery and mortars. 2 ESSEX casualties over the whole action amounted to eight killed and 54 wounded. Almost all the four hundred prisoners were taken by 2 SWB and 2 ESSEX and with the count of the dead and an estimate of the wounded, it was calculated that the Boche lost a grand total of seven hundred all ranks. We were relieved on 22 Jan. and returned to NIJMEGEN before taking over from the HALLAMSHIRES in the HAALDEREN sector on the 25th.

As we have already said, life in one sector of the "Island" salient is much like another, but it will refresh our memories and put the uninitiated in the picture if a few words are written about HAALDEREN.

CONNER UP! "He lives upon mouldy stewed prunes and dried cakes."

44

The sector derived its name from the small village in the centre and as time went by we agreed that it was the worst sector to look after. On the right ran the river WAAL well above ground level and contained by a bund. The only road was under small arms fire and approach had to be made by the "Jeep track" which was made out of the rubble from the destroyed houses. Whether the ground was frozen or feet deep in black mud, it was impossible to dig and one had to fight from the ruins of buildings and from cellars. Not a house remained whole and almost every room was fortified with sandbags and chests filled with dirt; in the small slits where windows used to be there was a weapon of some kind with the safety catch permanently at fire and a finger always on the trigger. The few houses not defended were mined and the unwary patrol from either side rarely left such a building in one piece. Contact with the enemy was as little as 100 yards and the whole Battalion area could be and was swept by Spandaus and other weapons. All the time patrols and snipers were active. Fortunately the Boche had a worse time than we did and the single German who left his position by day rarely returned; movement by half a dozen Boche brought down enough artillery and mortars to start a fair-sized attack. The little clusters of wrecked buildings earned their own names and instead of map references one spoke in terms of "Rotten Row", "Snipers Alley", "Spandau Joe the Third" etc etc. When things became a little monotonous, the chaps

ZETTEN "What the devil hast thou brought here?"

45

would play games to encourage the gullible enemy. A light would appear at night and when the Boche investigated, they would find a notice in German "Ever been had you B........s" and a couple of Brens on a flank would complete their discomforture. "S" Coy. would manhandle a 6-pounder in to the front line, blast the enemy at point-blank range and then discreetly retire before the answer came. HAALDEREN undoubtedly imposed a tremendous strain on all, particularly the lads in the most forward Coys. and only the imperturbable cheerfulness of the private soldier made extended duties and unceasing "stag" possible.

As winter drew to a close, the floods began to abate and people began to think of attacks once more. Even the Boche began to think about it for they showered us with leaflets, telling us of their new "Royal Tiger" that could swim like a submarine and would appear in our midst anytime with multiple guns firing in all directions. The leaflets had their purpose!! We even packed up once, ready to assist in the battles then taking place in the REICHSWALD FOREST but they struggled through without us and March still found 2 ESSEX on the "Island".

THE LAST ROUND.

The days of the salient were nearly at an end and on 2 April, when we were once more in HAALDEREN, 147 Bde. attacked through us and despite the masses of mines, quickly chased the Boche over the NEDER RIJN and cleared the enemy once and for all time out of the "Island". While the main British and American Armies were racing across Germany, plan after plan was made for the recapture of ARNHEM as a prelude to the final liberation of North West Holland. As the days passed each successive plan was abandoned until, in the darkness of 12/13 April, 2 GLOSTERS made the initial assault on ARNHEM from the East, crossing the IJSSEL RIVER in Buffaloes and assault boats. The recapture of ARNHEM in April 1945 can bear no comparison with the epic battle the "Red Devils" fought there in September 1944. The crossing of the IJSSEL was a difficult and praiseworthy feat; mines and concrete pillboxes abounded, but the enemy himself was in poor heart, particularly after being "Mattressed" with rocket bombs and plastered for days with artillery. The GLOSTERS had to fight hard for their bridgehead but 2 SWB and 2 ESSEX who followed met little physical opposition as we raced Westwards through the heart of the town, but on the high ground surrounding ARNHEM the Boche had masses of artillery and mortars and, with first-class, OPs, he had little difficulty in dropping his shells in the correct places. Captain Peter Butler, who subsequently died of his wounds, was one of a number of casualties. 2 ESSEX took only 145 prisoners in ARNHEM, the remainder fled Westwards leaving behind delayed action incendiaries to fire the town.

The final mopping up was completed within 36 hours of the initial assault and we were left to gape at the collossal defence preparations the Boche had made and we realised how lucky we had been. We saw the evidence of the tragedy of September 1944, the broken guns and equipment,

IJSSEL RIVER "In cradle of the rude imperious surge."

the little shallow slits the men had dug in a few seconds and from which they fought for days, until they died. We saw the little white crosses in corners of Dutch gardens, sometimes with a British name, often with an inscription such as "31 UNKNOWN BRITISH SOLDIERS" and perhaps on top of the cross would be a weather stained Red Beret which the Germans had placed there as a tribute to the cream of fighting men. The evidence of the closeness of the fighting was plain for all to see and, only a matter of yards from British Graves, were clusters of other white crosses with German names who, like their British opponents, had been buried in the trenches where they died.

Only one more attack remains. The lovely suburb of VELP was still in German hands but when we attacked on 16 April, we took nearly 100 prisoners without a single casualty. Disorganised, dispirited and lacking any orders, they offered not the slightest opposition as we swept through the town.

Returning to ARNHEM, we embarked in LCAs and LCMs on the 17th and sailed down the NEDER RIJN to RENKUM. In this completely ruined village we disembarked and marched into WAGENINGEN, again without opposition. Here Lt. Col. Butler DSO left us to return to a Battalion of his own Regiment and Lt. Col. E. S. Scott MBE took command. Between our own positions and those of the enemy ran the floodable valley of the river GREBBE and once more the battle became static, with extensive patrolling by both sides in which the enemy suffered far more heavily than we did.

We all knew that the end could not be long delayed, and the only doubt was whether the German Army in Holland would accept the order of their higher Command to surrender. This was answered on 25 April, when orders were received to cease offensive operations while discussions took place between the British and German Commanders to organise the transport of food into enemy-held Holland for the relief of the semi-starving inhabitants. On 5 May 1945 the German Army in Holland surrendered unconditionally and, two days later, we drove into occupied Holland along roads lined with cheering and flag-waving Dutch, whilst the enemy stayed in their billets and only their sentries were to be seen.

So we came to the end of a long long road. A road which started on the beaches of NORMANDY and finished, not as we would have hoped, in the heart of BERLIN, but in the centre of Holland. A road which twisted and turned and doubled backwards and forwards and where the POM-PADOURS only halted when they were ordered so to do and never at the dictate of the enemy. Along that road we said goodbye to 75% of the men that started the journey with us and many of those who joined as reinforcements. 10 Officers and 146 ORs were killed in action, 35 Officers and 526 Other Ranks suffered wounds of varying severity, 2 Officers and 85 ORs were reported missing and many others were evacuated through battle exhaustion and sickness. The price was a great one and one we must never forget, so that we may be constantly reminded that it is our duty to ensure that we and our children will never be called upon to make such a sacrifice again. It is in our hands and our hands alone to maintain a ruling body that will not allow the state of affairs which precipitated this war to recur again.

With this sobering thought, the POMPADOURS may look back with pride and a knowledge of unstinted endeavour, courage and achievement upon the campaign in North West Europe and we can return to our homes and say "We never once retreated". —

No more fitting conclusion to these pages is possible than the Special Order addressed to all ranks by Lt. Col. E. S. Scott MBE on 22 May 1945. It is reprinted overleaf:

ONE OF THE POMPADOURS
"Let the end try the man."

SPECIAL ORDER

BY

Lt. COL. E. S. SCOTT M. B. E.

"Now that the war in Europe is over and VE celebrations are dying down, I feel it is time for us all to pause for a moment and think of ourselves and how we helped to bring about the total and unconditional surrender of the German Nation. It has been my proud privilege to command the "POMPADOURS" during the final days and I wish personally to thank each Officer and OR for the part he played as a member of this very happy and successful team, which Lt. Col. Butler DSO did so much to build.

First of all let us never forget those who gave their lives for the cause and let us pray for their dependants. Let us remember those who were maimed for life and then thank God that we have come through safely.

In war, however good the troops are, they will not be successful and they will suffer unless their leaders are courageous and reliable. We were most fortunate in having first-class Coy. and Pl. Commanders, and so I particularly want to thank those Commanders and all Officers and NCOs who took their place when casualties occurred; and in no smaller way I want to thank the Junior leaders — the Section Commanders whose role is such a difficult and important one. Most of all shall I always remember the stout performance played by the private soldier. Many were the times when he knew little of the plan, but always could be relied upon to carry out his orders whether he was in a Rifle Coy. or in "S" Coy.

Finally I feel I must mention some of the specialists of HQ Coy. — The Signals who never let us down — The Drivers — The Stretcher Bearers — The Fitters — The Cooks and Watermen who have always been there when required and who get little rest — the Storeman — Eqpt. Repairer, Tailor, Armourer, Shoemakers and many more. All those have played their part and done it well.

It has been a great team and a very happy one and you have all held high the traditions of the "POMPADOURS". Well done! You have much to be proud of.

(Sd) E. S. Scott
Lt-Col.

BLA
22 May 45.

ROLL OF HONOUR
OFFICERS

Major G. M. M. L.	Petre
Capt P. E.	Butler
Capt P. J.	Chell
Capt N. F.	Harrison
Lieut. H. J.	Fradin
Lieut. D. W.	Grigg
Lieut. R. T.	Harris
Lieut. D. T.	Whitley
Lieut. R. E.	Miller
2/Lt T. G. L.	Cannon

OTHER RANKS

CSM W. Lane

CSM E. Roberts

Sjt. B. Burton.

Sjt. R. Flint.

Sjt. F. Myers.

Sjt. J. Pullen.

Sjt. W. Smith.

Cpl. E. Bucknill.

Cpl. W. Coe. MM

Cpl. G. Cutting.

Cpl. S. Enscoe.

Cpl. J. Flanagan.

Cpl. A. Hammerton.

Cpl. H. Haynes.

Cpl. J. Hollis.

Cpl. A. Hollands.

Cpl. G. Hull.

Cpl. J. Parton.

Cpl. A. Read.

Cpl. F. Roberts.

Cpl. J. Rogerson.

Cpl. H. Ruglys.

Cpl. C. Stanfield.

Cpl. J. Watts.

L/Cpl. B. Crofts.

L/Cpl. H. Colvill.

L/Cpl. A. Dodge.

L/Cpl. R. Gardiner.

L/Cpl. W. Hughes.

L/Cpl. A. Isaac.

L/Cpl. L. Keen.

L/Cpl. J. Procter.

L/Cpl. E. Randall.

L/Cpl. W. Seddon.

L/Cpl. W. Spooner.

L/Cpl. N. Shields.

L/Cpl. R. Saych.

L/Cpl. A. Shaw.

L/Cpl. J. Skerrett.

L/Cpl. H. Tempest.

L/Cpl. R. Willey.

L/Cpl. D. Wood.

L/Cpl. F. Williamson.

Pte. J. Allen.

Pte. A. Andrews.

Pte. H. Anderson.

Pte. G. Arkell.

Pte. F. Arundel.

Pte. H. Arstall.

Pte. W. Atkinson.

Pte. R. Attwood.

Pte. L. Averill.

Pte. M. Baird.

Pte. J. Baldwin.

Pte. E. Bambridge.

Pte. P. Bannatyne.

Pte. E. Barker.

Pte. F. Barnes.

Pte. C. Barton.

Pte. J. Beeston.

Pte. F. Bennett.

Pte. G. Bentley.

Pte. R. Bosley.

Pte. A. Bonnett.

Pte. J. Camfield.

Pte. P. Caplin.

Pte. W. Carter.

Pte. H. Catchpole.

Pte. T. Chambers.

Pte. A. Chapple.

Pte. J. Channing.

Pte. K. Clark.

Pte. J. Clark.

Pte. W. Clarke.

Pte. F. Commons.

Pte. A. Compton.

Pte. K. Cook.

Pte. F. Corder.

Pte. W. Cousins.

Pte. W. Cox.

Pte. J. Cranham.

Pte. E. Crump.

Pte. D. Davies.

Pte. J. Dean.

Pte. A. Dunn.

Pte. B. Dunlop.

Pte. H. Eatough.
Pte. N. Edgeley.
Pte. W. Edge.
Pte. E. Edwards.
Pte. F. Elliot.
Pte. H. Emmett.
Pte. W. Evans.
Pte. R. Finley.
Pte. A. Forman.
Pte. W. Garrett.
Pte. D. Genge.
Pte. J. Giddings.
Pte. H. Gilliland.
Pte. C. Ginn.
Pte. L. Goodspeed.
Pte. F. Goward.
Pte. A. Harrison.
Pte. R. Hewitt.
Pte. J. Howarth.
Pte. W. Hunt.
Pte. J. Hurley.
Pte. L. Irvin.
Pte. D. Jacobs.
Pte. A. Jay.
Pte. C. Joslin.
Pte. M. Kemp.
Pte. G. Keynes.
Pte. S. Kidman.
Pte. S. Layzell.
Pte. T. Lund.
Pte. J. Luxton.
Pte. H. Martin.
Pte. D. Marsh.
Pte. V. Marter.
Pte. P. Mc'Gowan ;
Pte. F. Menote.
Pte. A. Moore.
Pte. T. Moran.
Pte. A. Morley.
Pte. E. Morrill.
Pte. G. Mummery.
Pte. C. Nevill.

Pte. W. Nicol.
Pte. J. Pallett.
Pte. J. Parry.
Pte. D. Parry.
Pte. H. Pimblett.
Pte. K. Price.
Pte. N. Randle.
Pte. T. Rathe.
Pte. R. Richards.
Pte. L. Ridgewell.
Pte. A. Ring.
Pte. C. Robinson.
Pte. A. Roberts.
Pte. J. Rose.
Pte. A. Ross.
Pte. E. Rostron
Pte. J. Senft.
Pte. W. Senior.
Pte. A. Semmens.
Pte. K. Simpson.
Pte. D. Sherfield.
Pte. T. Shelley.
Pte. L. Shephard.
Pte. T. Smith.
Pte. G. Smith.
Pte. W. Sorby.
Pte. R. Stiles.
Pte. K. Stevens.
Pte. C. Strangleman.
Pte. S. Teague.
Pte. E. Townson.
Pte. T. Walton.
Pte. E. Watson.
Pte. W. Whittaker.
Pte. A. Whiteley.
Pte. C. Whymer.
Pte. A. Webb.
Pte. E. Webster.
Pte. T. Williams.
Pte. F. Willingham.
Pte. V. Woodward.
Pte. F. Wright.

„The dangers of the days but newly gone,
Whose memory is written on the earth
With yet appearing blood, and the examples
Of every minute's instance (present now)
Hath put us in these ill-beseeming arms:
Not to break peace, or any branch of it,
But to establish here a peace indeed,
Concurring both in name and quality."

King Henry IV Part II.

Lightning Source UK Ltd.
Milton Keynes UK
UKOW06f0616210217

294895UK00011B/46/P